Praise for

Naked in the Zendo

"Grace Schireson is a force of nature and a master of wild-ass Zen. She has studied in Japan and America with Soto and Rinzai teachers. Schireson Roshi spent years investigating koans with the Rinzai master Keido Fukushima Roshi and received Dharma transmission from the Soto master Sojun Mel Weitsman. *Naked in the Zendo* draws upon turning points in her life to show critical aspects of our emerging Western Zen. This is a wonderful book. I highly recommend it."

JAMES ISHMAEL FORD
author of *Introduction to Zen Koans*

"This is a book about the heart of Zen practice, how to awaken to vast awareness and then engage that awareness in transforming distress into freedom and contentment in everyday life. *Naked in the Zendo* combines pithy Zen koans with illuminating stories from the author's personal life as a wife and mother, from her adventures in Zen training in the US, and as a woman practicing in an all-male monastery in Japan."

JAN CHOZEN BAYS
author of *Mindfulness on the Go*

"You're not sitting on your cushion, says Grace Schireson, to get good at meditation, but to transform your life. And not necessarily through the dramatic moments of realization we usually associate with Zen, but with the flowering of awareness into those seemingly little everyday acts of kindness and responsiveness. When I was just starting out in my own practice, I might not have had the sense to recognize and appreciate such undramatic wisdom. I hope *Naked in the Zendo* will inspire this awareness for both new and seasoned practitioners."

BARRY MAGID
author of *Ending the Pursuit of Happiness*

"In these clear-headed, clear-hearted stories of American Zen (serious Zen framed by an American sensibility), Grace Schireson will grab your attention and open your awareness. Awareness is the hero of these stories and Schireson is your guide as she tells you what to hold on to and what to let go of when you engage your deepest intention to wake up to reality. Schireson is a wise, funny, and uniquely feminist American Zen teacher whose approach to practice will enrich everyone."

POLLY YOUNG-EISENDRATH
author of *Love between Equals*

NAKED
IN THE
ZENDO

Stories of Uptight Zen,

Wild-Ass Zen,

and Enlightenment

Wherever You Are

GRACE SCHIRESON

Foreword by Joan Halifax

SHAMBHALA
Boulder
2019

SHAMBHALA PUBLICATIONS, INC.
4720 Walnut Street
Boulder, Colorado 80301
www.shambhala.com

Chapter 8, "Too Much *Mu*," was first published in *The Book of Mu: Essential Writings on Zen's Most Important Koan*, edited by James Ishmael Ford and Melissa Myozen Blacker (Wisdom Publications, 2011).

9 8 7 6 5 4 3 2 1

First Edition

Printed in the United States of America

⊗ This edition is printed on acid-free paper that meets the American National Standards Institute z39.48 Standard.
♻ Shambhala Publications makes every effort to print on recycled paper. For more informtion please visit www.shambhala.com

Shambhala Publications is distributed worldwide by Penguin Random House, Inc., and its subsidiaries.

Designed by Kate Huber-Parker

LIBRARY OF CONGRESS CATALOGING-IN-PUBLICATION DATA
Names: Schireson, Grace Jill, author.
Title: Naked in the Zendo: stories of uptight Zen, wild-ass Zen, and enlightenment wherever you are / Grace Schireson.
Description: Boulder: Shambhala, 2019. |
Includes bibliographical references.
Identifiers: LCCN 2019007664 | ISBN 9781611806564 (pbk.: alk. paper)
Subjects: LCSH: Schireson, Grace Jill. | Buddhist women—United States—Biography.
Classification: LCC BQ984.C47 A3 2019 | DDC 294.3/927092—dc23
LC record available at https://lccn.loc.gov/2019007664

This book is for my grandchildren Jacob, Isabel, and Olivia Lyell Schireson, and especially for my youngest granddaughter, Gala Amador Schireson, who will definitely not be left out.

Contents

Foreword

Buddhist women's voices can tend to be subdued in and sometimes even absent from public conversation. Not so with Roshi Grace Schireson. Her forthrightness, her strength, her humor, and her wisdom are threads that weave this marvelous book into a powerful tapestry of insight, inspiration, and teaching. This book explores the powerful territory of awareness—not awareness in the romantic sense but awareness as it opens itself in the context of one's everyday life.

Brave and true, Roshi Grace pushes the reader to let go of the pretenses and pretending that shield us from who we really are. She wants us to recognize our innate wisdom and to actualize compassion that is not based on pity but on courage—the courage to look and the courage to see.

Filled with funny and startling stories, this book is also bursting with wisdom and has a special flavor of brave kindness. I know, from my own experience, that writing about "awareness" is no small task, but Grace has managed to break open this hard subject with skill and wit.

As I proceeded through this marvelous book, I found myself not only smiling from her humor but also nodding in agreement with her very sharp analysis of the meditative experience. Her insight about discovering sentience as a child was fascinating, as she became aware of the mutuality between beings and things. She points out that meditation practice is a way that we can amplify our experience of awareness, reveal it, and sharpen it. She then helps us understand that awareness can be circulated through our relationships, not only to others but to all of life, and thus, awareness can arise naturally, spontaneously through the fabric of our whole and precious life and the granular details therein.

Her stories of meeting Suzuki Roshi open a window through which we view the lifelong changes that come from meeting one's teacher. The hook had sunk deep and she was caught by Suzuki Roshi's tenderness and her own developing awareness.

As Grace's friends will attest and her book reflects, she is not just a seeker of truth in the conventional sense; rather, she demands truth from herself and others. She stands not only in love but also alongside justice. Her practice is focused on accountability and responsibility in these changing and fraught times. She has learned hard lessons as a woman and as a post-modern human. She has taken those lessons to heart and is bringing them to her wider Zen community and the wider world. A leader in ending gender bias not only in Buddhism but also in Eastern and Western society, she teaches that her own journey with discovering, amplifying, and circulating awareness is not just a personal enhancement program but is also about ending suffering in our time.

I read her book and felt love and awe. This is a book that is both intimate and prophetic.

ROSHI JOAN HALIFAX

Introduction

Naked in the Zendo is a book about how to develop and engage undifferentiated or vast awareness in the midst of everyday life experiences. The *zendo* is the room in which you meditate. Even though we are fully clothed, how do we drop the ego's protective covering and allow ourselves full exposure to awareness? You may wish to uncover innate wisdom and compassion through meditative practice, but there is always the danger of trying to look good or smart, to try to do a practice right that engages a protective layer of ego. Exposing the ego's cover-up is the task of spiritual practice, and this book describes how the mind may engage awareness to encounter its ego-driven cover-ups whether in the zendo or in the midst of life experiences.

Awareness is a vast topic; and it can be defined by two aspects: essence of mind and contents of mind. Essence of mind is that which is aware of what we are thinking, feeling, sensing, and experiencing. Content of mind is the specific thoughts, feelings, and impulses that arise within essence or naked awareness. It is the essence of mind, our own undifferentiated awareness, that may observe what arises in our own mind in any moment. Like the sky, this essence exists and functions whether we choose to notice it or not. While we may not increase this awareness, we may strengthen our relationship to it.

We develop our own relationship to awareness or essence of mind in a variety of ways. We have formal spiritual practices, done privately or in community, such as meditation, prayer, and chanting. Everyday life encounters can also be an opportunity to engage awareness. We can stop in the midst of our lives to allow awareness to guide us. As ninth-century Zen Master Joshu taught, from *The Recorded Sayings of Zen Master Joshu*: "You are used by the twenty-four hours, I use the twenty-four hours." This book describes how I used the twenty-four hours to deepen my awareness practice over fifty years of meditation and relationships. I identify four stages of developing awareness practice or how the mind may reflect itself:

1. Discovery: When I first observed awareness during childhood, I become conscious that I was looking out at a world that was alive with sentience. I was watching life, but it was also watching me.

2. Amplification: Through meditation practice, I learned how to focus on my relationship to this awareness—to strengthen or amplify my relationship to awareness.

3. Circulating awareness: As I practiced becoming aware of awareness in my Zen community, I found it connected to people, feelings, and even to the food I cooked during meditation retreats. Learning how to pay attention to awareness, even while emotionally engaged, helped me to exchange old habits for wisdom in relationships.

4. Awareness arising spontaneously: After decades of awareness exercises at Zen centers, I found that awareness could arise spontaneously in my family relationships and daily life.

These stages describe developing awareness and actualizing it in everyday life.

In part 1 I share how early in my life my own view included an accidental encounter with awareness as a spacious relationship with God. As a young adult, I reencountered that space when I met Shunryu Suzuki Roshi. At the time of the meeting, I was twenty years old and a junior at UC Berkeley, and I had the commonly held young-adult view of my own omniscience. Shunryu Suzuki Roshi was a Zen teacher who had been teaching San Francisco seekers for more than ten years. He and his followers founded San Francisco Zen Center and Tassajara, the first Zen monastery in the West. This part shares my personal experience meeting him and how meeting Suzuki Roshi's spacious mind changed my life.

In part 2 I travel to the source of what I am studying: how to amplify my awareness in meditation. Rabbis may train in Israel, chefs may train in Paris, Catholics may visit the Vatican. When you are trying to learn a skill, how do you enter it authentically? How do you know what applies today or what is bound up with previous and foreign cultural norms? For example, a friend studied Italian architecture, and here in California he replicated a house found centuries ago in the Italian alps. An Italian friend commented on the window size: "The reason the windows are so small is that the owners in the Italian alps were taxed on the size of the windows—not the size of the house." Did small windows add to the architectural and functional experience of the house? Studying tradition in another culture may help us find the core activities that deepen our practice. What do we keep, what do we adapt, and what do we throw out?

In returning to the source, I encounter the gender discrimination built into Japanese Zen, but I also find a tenderness and caring that I hadn't yet sensed in Western Zen. I share my personal struggle as a Western Zen woman meeting and subjecting myself to the traditional patriarchal monastic Japanese Zen establishment. Misunderstandings and adaptations were necessary on both sides and were sometimes jarring to participants in this relationship. Even though I was not (technically) allowed to practice in the male monastic setting, I did just that through the compassion and flexibility of individual Japanese Zen teachers and through my own ability to both fit in and find my space. I was guided and pulled forward by my pursuit of awareness. In Zen practice we call this "Way seeking mind."

In part 3 I share how practicing with friends, family, and peers deepens our understanding. While we can read about Zen in books, and we can practice in a foreign land, in order to make a practice our own we need to find familiar settings in which our egotistical habits arise. As we see ourselves with our peers, and we practice a form of transformation, we can integrate training with our lives.

This part describes how individual personalities, friendships, and group practices affect our awareness. Zen centers and monasteries, and the unique individuals who practice within them, expose both the compassion and the creativity of Zen practice in our native tongue. These are useful examples of how the Buddhist Way changes and how our awareness deepens in meeting the Way on our own turf. This part describes how Zen circulates awareness in our body-mind equipment through relationships and rituals.

Finally, in part 4 I share how awareness has penetrated my home and family life. I have learned to sense awareness and trust it to roam freely in my life—I listen for instructions from this wisdom. This part describes how awareness affects my parenting and my grandparenting. After formally developing my connection to awareness, I began to sense the space in my own mind where my family could grow into becoming themselves. Beyond formal training in awareness practices, I share how awareness has transformed my view of life problems in family and community Zen at home.

I have practiced mistake after mistake, and I was surprised to see the awareness I developed in formal Zen practice making decisions for me at home. Its effects seeped into my everyday life. From these fifty years of Zen adventures, I have distilled principles from which I teach myself and my students. "You are *not* practicing meditation on the cushion to get good at doing meditation. You are practicing meditation so it transforms your life," I tell them. Or, "Just let meditation into your body-mind equipment; it knows how to do what it knows how to do with you." Meditation practice is like a seed that takes root in your body-mind equipment; as it grows, as you practice, it finds its own way to transform your awareness. With spiritual practice, like meditation, you become more conscious, more compassionate, and more liberated.

My Japanese Rinzai Zen teacher, Keido Fukushima Roshi, was asked by one of my students, "What is the most important thing (in Zen)?" Roshi answered, "Watching your mind." With what does the mind watch itself? How do we expand the mind so that it reflects its own image? How do we create a transformative space in the mind? We don't use the mind's energy to try to overcome negative habits, taking meditation on the cushion as a drug and expecting ourselves to just *stop* it. We don't overcome our negative habits by insisting that we follow the precepts "or else." If simply demanding change solved our negative tendencies, we would be well on our way to having a perfect world. So how do we change? How do we transform the mind and its afflictive emotions that cause so much suffering to ourselves and others?

In this book I approach this question by revealing my own mind at work through the course of my life in challenging moments. I watch the mind watching itself. Awareness is aware of awareness. As I watch, I have seen how my mind may reflect itself in an expanded space. This experience has increased my options and the directions in which I may venture. Throughout this book I share how this self-reflection affected me—how Zen opened my eyes, my heart, and my relationships and uncovered my hidden defenses.

I have learned that Westerners, including myself, tend to come to Zen meditation as if it were a pharmaceutical. If only I can get the right dosage from the right teacher, I can take this medicine and be transformed. But I have learned otherwise—much of the transformation occurs off the cushion, in the midst of life's challenges. The watching is like washing the mind in its own reflection, breath by breath. We find the space in the mind to mix Buddhist teachings together with life in this moment. We pour practice into our difficulties, blending them in the container of our awareness and living out the fusion we create.

While I accidently entered expanded awareness as a child, I found later in life that meditation strengthened my relationship to awareness and allowed me to turn toward it intentionally. The meditation cushion is a laboratory for calming the mind and learning how to return to this space. When we pour the practice into daily life with its joys and suffering, we are infused with its awareness and we become one with the practice in a more aware life. Then meditation is not something outside of ourselves but rather the space within, to which we return for healing and for an appropriate response—a response that meets the moment squarely, without making it worse. If we return to watching our mind and breath when walking, driving, waiting in line, being criticized, our whole life will be transformed. In other words, we need to trust the practice with our entire life.

This book intends to reveal, through a window on my life, my first encounters with awareness, how my own awareness sought out meditation training, how this training moved from being foreign and outside of me, and finally, how being aware of awareness takes on a life of its own, expressing itself in every aspect of a practitioner's life. The question remains: Who sought whom? Did awareness guide me, or did "I" pursue it?

We don't need to seek out each bad habit; we just need to keep becoming nakedly and lucidly aware of awareness. In this way, we enter the great space of awareness and let the difficulties free themselves—like smoke dissipating in a big sky. Let us find this space and live in it. Awareness practice for me applies an essential Buddhist teaching principle: All defilements are self-liberating in the great space of awareness.

May it be so.

Part One

Mind as Sky

Spiritual Energy and the Light of Awareness

Awareness is the self-reflective property of the mind that can grow in brightness, focus, depth, and quality. Children can find this spacious mind accidentally; many of us can recall these early experiences. Suddenly our mind becomes as vast as the sky. We are not caught by circumstances; our view has expanded. This part describes my earliest experiences of finding a spacious and expanded mind. First, it just happened on its own. Then the experience occurred through meeting with Suzuki Roshi and Zen practice. Finally, this essential function—developing my relationship to awareness—became my quest.

The first step in the process of finding awareness has been described in traditional Zen texts. Wherever we look historically, we find philosophers, scholars, and other visionaries trying to understand the mind. The well-respected Chinese Zen monk Yunmen (862–949) taught his students how to work with awareness. In case 86 of the *Blue Cliff Record*, Yunmen said, "Everyone has their own light. If you look for it, you can't find it." In other words, the light can illuminate your mind, but with an idea in your mind that you will "get" this light, it does not appear. When you are after something, you create a mind-set of activity, of mental commotion—a separated self that is looking for something. One part of your mind has separated and is chasing after a prized goal. This is like a dog chasing his own tail—lots of activity, but the goal is not accomplished. This is like creating ripples when reaching for a stick in the water; what you are trying to reach gets farther away. This is why children can have a spontaneous experience of the mind lighting up and expanding. They are not yet trying to achieve anything in particular.

Actually, the light appears on its own when you *become*, rather than pursue, a unified presence; this is why Yunmen cautioned against seeking it. When you settle into your own being, your own breath, your own body—when you unite body, breath, and mind—you connect with your self. Naturally, your mind reflects the light of awareness. This light allows you to watch your own thoughts as they arise. Through finding the spaciousness, light, or luminosity in your mind, you can observe the subtle movements of the mind without being pulled around to act on them. You enjoy a sense of grounded connection while just watching what arises in your mind—no grasping and no averting. You develop an unfiltered intimacy with what is actually going through your mind and to the circumstances to which your mind is reacting.

1

Beginning with What Is It?

As a young child, I remember watching my mind open. Surely as we grow up and mature, we glimpse the possibility to view our own thoughts, emotions, limitations, and strengths. As adults, we try to step back and consider our mind objectively; we are especially motivated to consider our mind when we feel uncomfortable. Watching our thoughts and emotions requires us to see ourselves in a larger context that includes others and our circumstances and conditions. This is our relationship to sky-mind, or awareness. I remember entering this space early in my life, and I believe it helped me through some dark times.

I am the second daughter in a family with two girls and a boy. As a middle child, I received many things secondhand. Some things were worn, and some things, like my mother, were worn out. My sister is two and a half years older than me, which means she would have been about twenty months old when my mother became pregnant with me. My younger brother was conceived when I was five months old. A fourth child would have quickly followed my younger brother if my mother had not found a back-alley abortion. As a teenager, I heard about how she was left weak and bleeding.

My father died when I was six, leaving my mother unprepared to cope financially. She went back to work right away with little infrastructure to care for us children. My brother was sent to live with my grandmother—another terrible loss for me. I learned to rely primarily on myself and my older sister during my early chaotic years. We know that children find ways to survive hardships and an absence of support. One way is through siblings and invisible friends or forces. Through my sister I found ways to feel connected. But I also found an invisible force toward which I could turn—my own awareness and presence. In my world, I was conversing with God.

My sister, as the eldest, had a special role in the family; her guidance and her castoffs—advice, clothes, toys, but especially books—were influential and meaningful. She had skills that she passed on to me as well. She taught me to read before I went to school. I remember the lessons she gave me ahead of kindergarten, and I remember one of her books most of all. It was a beautiful leather-bound Bible—it read from right to left—that my paternal uncle Arnold had brought back from Israel in 1950. I remember what its leather felt like, and I remember the feel of the cover embossed in gold.

Uncle Arnold was a jazz musician who toured the world performing for much of his life. He started with Glenn Miller and other big bands when he was sixteen. He had purchased this Bible in Israel, while performing on a tour, and he gave it to my sister. She, after all, could read, and she, as the eldest, received all special gifts. But she showed no interest in this book and put it away in her drawer with other hidden treasures. I looked into this drawer when she was out of the room—sneaking peeks at her private life. No wonder my family nickname was Sneaky.

The beautiful leather-bound Bible was tucked in with little-girl clothing all around it. I opened the drawer and looked over my shoulder. Sis was nowhere to be seen. I soon lost interest in whatever other treasures I was hunting. I picked up the Bible and turned it over, trying to find the right way to examine it since I could not yet read. I opened it and saw the printed words, which I now suspect were Hebrew. As I held the Bible, I heard a heavenly choir. Even though no one had spoken to me about this book, I felt its power. For a moment I stood transfixed, taking in the amazing message I was receiving. This book mattered; this book was different. This book held secrets—secrets that would wait but that would continue to matter to me. Right then I needed to tuck the book back into its hidden home among little-girl clothing. I knew I would return to this message later.

I remember that moment as if it were right now. I feel the power of the heavenly choir. The wonderment I felt, I feel today. The book's singing power in my hands has inspired me throughout life. I was bathed in the power. In considering your own life, can you remember what called you and how you stay true to that calling? My life did not follow that book; it followed my experience holding the book, the power of what was yet to be revealed.

So my spiritual life did not begin with meditation practice. It began when I realized that the universe was holding me and singing to me its amazing song. Since I went to a Jewish Sunday school, I called that presence God, and I also knew the conversation with Him was always available to me. I merged my experience holding that evocative leather-bound Bible, the Israeli Old Testament, with what I learned in Sunday school. The Sunday school lessons were about how certain men had conversations with God. I just assumed I could have that same relationship. I could speak and be heard; He would answer me. I knew that I was with God and that He was watching me, waiting to converse.

My family did not continue my religious training; it became too expensive after my father's death. But in high school

I went to synagogue with a Jewish girls' social group. I had joined the group for the parties with Jewish boys, but I loved my time at temple in the same way I had as a small child. On the rare occasions when I went to temple, I found that the shared calling out to God, the singing, amplified my sense of being in dialogue. I found being among practicing Jews inspiring. We were all calling out, we were all singing, and we were all being held in God's presence. This feeling was embodied joy. I did not think these thoughts; I felt them in my body.

When I learned to meditate, I felt the same joy in my body, and I felt that I belonged to a vast space. I recognized a connection to something far beyond my small self. In my first spiritual experience, as a four-year-old middle daughter, I felt held in a vast context. I was in contact with a space that held everything—a space that could answer my questions. My relationship to it allowed me to have deep conversations when I was overwhelmed by events. I had such a conversation the night my father died.

One night my father did not come home from work; he was killed in a car accident by a drunk driver. As a six-year-old, I began by wondering how I had somehow caused his death. Yet the space opened, and within the vast space available to me I was able to consider the facts. I reviewed the events and my own activities in my conversation with God. I considered that my father had gone to work, that he had driven home, that a (drunk) driver had hit his car, and that he had died. As I reviewed my potential involvement in his death within God's view, I concluded that I hadn't caused this car accident. My father's work life was beyond me, his commute was beyond me, and the activity of the drunk driver was also beyond my control.

In contrast, and with much sadness as an adult, I learned that my brother, upon his own review, concluded that our father's death was his fault. My brother suffered the guilt of his imagined patricide for much of his life. Because our father had been physically abusive with my brother, he had, in fact, wished our father dead. I had received Father's spankings; my brother received his stranglings. He concluded that his wish had come true. Was it the fourteen-month age difference, the intense physical abuse that engendered his explicit wish, or my conversations with God that allowed me to understand my role through a larger view? I knew what I had and hadn't done, and I knew I had not killed my father.

I didn't know exactly what death meant, but as time passed I intuited that his death meant my father would never come home again. I was too young to understand what *never* meant and too young to work through my loss. I held a secret conviction that I would find him somewhere. I held this belief unconsciously, until I found myself scanning a group of pedestrians in San Francisco, examining their faces as they crossed the street in front of me. I was looking for him, thinking he had just not returned home to Los Angeles. Maybe he was elsewhere. By then I was eighteen, and I connected more fully with my loss. Watching myself watching others, I could see the child I had been. And I could see that child entering adulthood missing her father.

Spiritual practice, however it develops, provides ways for us to see ourselves in a larger context. As the medieval Christian mystic Meister Eckhart (1260–1328) said in one of his sermons, "The eye through which I see God is the same eye through which God sees me; my eye and God's eye are one eye, one seeing, one knowing, one love." Whether we refer to this view as not knowing, awareness, space, or God, our view may expand to allow a different perception of our circumstances. When we see ourselves within a vast contextual web, this is one aspect of expanded awareness. We are not a solo combatant, railing against circumstances. We can see how we are all moving in vast space with surprising connections. The difficulty we encounter has space in which it can untangle itself.

Using the eye with which we are seen, using the space within which we find ourselves, we can move in a less confined sense of space, time, and self. Our growth as humans, our ability to see our own limitations and strengths, depends on a larger context, a space in which we can turn around to see ourselves. We can see our lives, held in a bigger world; we can let go of hindrances and watch our dreams unfolding in the vast sky-mind. A Sikh leader once told me that Sikhs meditate on God. He asked me what the object of meditation was for Zen practitioners. With a pause I answered, "We meditate on the mind of God."

2

MY FATHER, MY BROTHER, AND THE WOLF DOG

The Three Dimensions of Time

Memories can open like doors connecting past, present, and future. We can bring a past memory to life, and we can shift its previous meaning to be seen as something else in the present moment. I learned how malleable my childhood memories were when I considered some of my last impressions of my father. The childhood memories became something else as I reencountered them as an adult. The space of awareness allowed me to turn and face my father as an adult.

My memories of my father are limited. I was six when he died. Thanks to my brother's mischievousness, I retain one strong memory of my father and the wolf dog. This dog was well known in my early childhood neighborhood fables, a dog believed to be part wolf and mostly vicious. We children spoke of this dog in hushed tones. Whose dog was it? Where did it live? Was it part wolf? None of us knew the real story of the wolf dog. Most of us had never even seen him.

On a warm summery day, my four-year-old brother told me he had found a really cute dog near our yard. My little brother was not known for his strict adherence to safety or facts. I asked, "It's not the wolf dog is it?" He assured me it was not the wolf dog; it was a different, friendly dog. Being a curious, five-year-old dog lover, I agreed to go with him to see it. We went out the back door, so as not to be noticed or questioned. Within a short distance, we were out in an empty lot filled with tumbleweeds, hard dirt, and no fences—a secret place of children's play.

Soon enough I spotted a dog in front of me. It looked neither friendly nor playful. I thought that I must be face-to-face with the mythical creature—the wolf dog. I looked around for my brother, but he had already run away. As I turned to walk back home, the dog caught up with me and bit me on the right thigh—just below my buttocks. I felt the bite, and from an unknown somewhere I received instructions: "Don't run, but slowly walk away." I did just that, realizing that my situation had become somewhat precarious.

I headed back to my house without running or looking back. I entered the house through the same side door. I heard running water and headed toward it—ready to discuss the wolf dog and my bleeding leg with an adult. Unlike my little brother, I understood danger. Feeling blood running down my leg compelled me to talk over our misadventure with a parent. The sound of water running turned out to be my father shaving.

So I approached him, my earnest little self still enacting the calm necessary to escape the wolf dog's biting attack. "The wolf dog bit me," I said quietly, being careful not to get my brother in trouble. My father continued his shaving without looking at me, and said, "Don't make up stories." I understood his meaning, but clearly he had not understood mine. So I said, "No, really. Look." I turned my thigh toward him, hiked up my shorts, and revealed the bloody bite mark.

Turning toward my father and away from the view of my leg, I watched my father's face in the mirror he was using to shave. His color went from pink to white, beginning with his forehead, all the way down to his chin. I watched the color drain from his face while he screamed my mother's name, "Jean!" My mother came immediately, examined the bite, and called the doctor. I remember being seen by a local doctor, a discussion of rabies shots, and no shots being given. I remember jokes about whether my leg was delicious or not. But mostly I will never forget that vivid, child's-eye view of shock draining the color from my father's face.

Thirty-five years later, when I did Gestalt therapy to explore my childhood loss of my father, I was asked to recall my most vivid memory of him. I remembered his reaction to the wolf dog—his appearance, his face changing color, his concern for me, and his distress over my injury. With this recollection my therapist asked me to request his presence and speak to him. From our wolf dog encounter, I launched myself into that dramatic moment. My questions for him were: Where had he gone? Why had he abandoned me? What did he have to say to me now? The memory became present tense. I spoke to my father, and he answered me. In that encounter my understanding of our relationship evolved. Our relationship changed in the therapist's office. I now understood his death as an adult—speaking to an adult.

What is the past? What is the present? The complex nature of time does not just pass and fade away, teaches Japanese Zen priest and philosopher Dogen (1200–1253) in *The Time Being (Uji)*. Psychologists teach that the unconscious has no past tense, and the body keeps score. Each moment is alive; each moment is intimately connected to our lives and all other moments. However, when a memory is accessed with awareness, the experience becomes alive again. Dogen writes in *The Time Being*,

Do not think that time merely flies away. Do not see flying away as the only function of time. If time merely flies away, you would be separated from time. The reason you do not clearly understand the time-being is that you think of time only as passing. In essence, all things in the entire world are linked with one another as moments.

What does this mean for all of us? When we enter a moment of awareness, it affects our life. Even when it is a past moment, it is not a historical event that is complete and cast in stone. If we bring our full attention to a moment, it exists in our current life and it connects us to future possibilities. This book's introduction mentioned the teaching about negative mental states: "All defilements are self-liberating in the great space of awareness." This applies to painful memories, longings, a sense of loss or trauma. If we can muster presence of mind, if we experience the great space of awareness, we find that our path leads from suffering to freedom.

Time can exist as past, present, or future. Practicing full attention, presence in this moment, we can encounter a past event that becomes alive as now in the great space of awareness. By allowing the past moment its life in awareness, we can change our future. What was held in place as a painful or traumatic memory becomes alive; it is changed and affects our future. The flow of time is forward and backward. How do we create the space in which past becomes present and transforms our future?

Meditation, prayer, and therapy allow us a space within which we may relive a past experience, either traumatic or inspirational. The past is experienced with the same intensity and emotional tone as our initial experience. But the space of awareness is bigger. We are no longer limited to the close-up view—the view limited by age, intensity, or lack of experience.

We are no longer the overwhelmed witness. We feel the space, the room to consider and move. The view has expanded and changed. Perhaps it had hardened over the years. But we can engage willingness to feel the space around a past experience, the space within which we can more fully experience that moment. Then our view is no longer constrained by our past limitations, our youthful inexperience, or our sense of power- lessness. When we are fully present, we may find and enter the great space of awareness. However, it takes practice to come to know this space and to enter it willfully. Within this space we can find a different relationship to loss, pain, and trauma, allowing such emotions to dissipate and release themselves in that expanded space of awareness.

3

The Body of Truth

I was a latchkey kid in the days before that term existed. With my father dead, my mother working, and no childcare, we three siblings went to school and came home to an empty apartment. As we became teenagers, our anger bubbled up along with our unique interests. My brother's interest was money, my sister's was friends, and mine was using academic achievement as my ticket out of my unhappy surroundings. This goal brought with it adopting a mocking, sarcastic, pseudo-intellectual persona at home and at school.

One of my mother's fixations was cleanliness, and she demanded my sister's and my participation in housecleaning. Her fury would emerge in angry insults over small infractions such as a single dish left in the sink. She seemed to take our lack of full participation in her demanding standards of tidiness as a personal attack, and so she often responded with personal insults. Such was the case one Saturday when she came into the bedroom I shared with my sister. Saturdays were especially tense since she was home from work supervising our thorough housecleaning.

My mother entered our room and in her angry tone pronounced her disappointment at the messiness: "The problem is that you two girls are a couple of shits." Using my sarcastic and superior professorial tone, I responded, "That's it, Mother! You have solved this problem. In fact, the room is messy just because we are a couple of shits." While ostensibly I was agreeing, my mother recognized sass when she heard it.

Mother picked up a plastic attachment to the vacuum cleaner and threw it at me. My defiance continued as I stared right at her, not even putting up my hands to shield my face. Her aim was better than expected at twelve feet, and the hard, angular object struck me just below the right eye. With the immediate pain and blood, my attitude instantly shifted from defiant to needy. "I need ice," I requested urgently. However, my sister was trying to hit my mother at that point, and my mother was trying to protect herself. So I went to get my own ice for my emerging black eye.

When the fighting had stopped, and my sister had left to hang out with her friends, I sat face-to-face with my mother at the kitchen table. Tearfully, I said, "I know you didn't mean to hurt me." She shook her head and looked me in my one good eye, "Yes, I did mean to hurt you. I wanted to hurt you." I remember those words, and I remember my mind opening in astonishment. I had never consciously wanted to hurt anyone. I assumed hurting another person was accidental for all. I realized, in that icy moment, that my view had just expanded. I was astonished rather than angry. I realized that because something was true for me, it was not necessarily universally true. This realization would stay with me.

Trauma, damaging as it is, may also provide the ground for opening the mind. When the body is in pain and shock, the thinking mind can quiet and open to a vivid experience of vastness. A moment of suffering can free the mind to realize the truths of human existence: our interconnectedness and our impermanence. My mother's life and mine were intertwined. Her pain, her short fuse, her own traumatic childhood were also mine. She had also gifted me with her brutal honesty. As I shared this trauma later in my life, a wise friend pointed out my mother's lack of pretense. I processed the pain and trauma along with the realization that honesty was her most precious gift.

Brutal honesty was a guiding light for me later in my own parenting. I believed that my own sons would need to know the difference between pretend and reality to make important decisions in their lives. While I watched other parents and grandparents "make nice," covering over mean remarks or harsh actions, I saw the child's confusion resulting from that approach. While one needs to temper the level of harsh details to suit a child's age and development, covering up or lying about uncomfortable facts is not helpful to a child's developing moral compass. How much more would I have suffered if my mother had lied to me and said, "It was an accident. I didn't mean to hurt you." It may have been comforting in the moment, but I would have missed an important lesson. Humans struggle with many different levels of rage, fear, and impulse control.

As a teenager, I had another realization. Courage, rebelliousness, and a sense of invulnerability would not be sufficient to protect my body from injury. In Zen training I came across an important teaching: "Save the body, it is the fruit of many lifetimes." While the practice of fearlessness and a samurai spirit pervade Zen training, it seems that we can work on developing awareness while alive in this body. While spiritual teachings suggest life after death, so far, we have not established how humans can practice without a body. This very body is the place of practice and realization. And from my encounter with my mother's rage I began to understand that I needed to protect myself, my body, in order to continue living.

Later in life, when I practiced in Japan with Tofukuji abbot Fukushima Roshi, he affirmed the necessity of practicing completely but with scrupulous truthfulness about the body's limitations, as I will share more about later. Even though I had early on learned about physical limitations, I believed that Zen spirit meant pushing on without giving in to them. Fukushima Roshi reminded me of the need for my own self-care. I taught my students this principle in these words: "You are the Dharma vessel, just as you revere the Buddha's teaching, you should protect and nourish your own body." Physical trauma and hardship can open your mind to your unique place in the universe. But do not ignore danger and pain when navigating life experiences.

4

ZEN WILL GET YOU HIGH

I met Suzuki Roshi in 1967 when I was a student at UC Berkeley. I had been encouraged to meet him by my sister's best friend. Leslie's unique recommendation: "There's a guy in San Francisco who can teach you how to get high without drugs." To a hippie flower child of the '60s, this was a claim worth investigating. How far out! What if this claim were true? My sister and I made an appointment to meet with Suzuki Roshi on a Saturday afternoon. Without knowing anything about Zen Buddhism, we were about to step into deep water. It took me a while to realize how wet I had become.

My sister and I rode our motorcycles across the Bay Bridge from Berkeley to San Francisco Zen Center on our psychedelic quest. We made a brief stop at an import store to further decorate ourselves with large hoop earrings. We were well made up; I wore a miniskirt, tights, shoes similar to those worn by Dorothy in *The Wizard of Oz*, and a necklace with bells that jingled when I walked. And so, we appeared to an amused Suzuki Roshi, who answered our apprehensive knock at the Zen center's front door. Suzuki Roshi knew who we were and why we had come before we said a word.

Suzuki Roshi had been teaching Zen to hippies in San Francisco for a decade. Part of the hippie credo was an abundant confidence in our worldview. I was imbued with the belief that I had the most profound worldview ever to be known by a living being. And so, we entered the world of Zen. Without ceremony, Suzuki Roshi led us upstairs to the zendo meditation space. He showed us to the meditation tatami platform and motioned us over to the black round and rectangular cushions—the *zafus* and *zabutons*—perfectly spaced with yellow woven tatami mats. The sight of this orderly, clean space sent a wave of aesthetic appreciation through my mind. Was this how you got high? He instructed us to bow to the cushion and then to bow away. He explained that we needed to bow to the spirits sitting on the cushion, because when we took our places to meditate we would be displacing them. I was already excited about how far out this little old man could be, and I was looking forward to meeting these meditating spirits and their mysterious power to get me high.

Instead of meeting the invisible spirits, I received my first Zen meditation (zazen) instructions. We spent what seemed like two hours meditating with him over the next ten minutes. The discomfort in my undisciplined mind was running away with me. Would this work? Would I get high? What was taking so long? I was able to put aside my discomfort because I knew the goodies and my high were coming soon. When we finished our meditation, we turned toward Suzuki Roshi for our personal map to getting high.

He knew he had our full attention. Although his English was poor, I have a feeling he made it even worse to ensure we listened carefully. We hung on his every word. He began with words that promised us our place in the high zone—the ticket to getting high from Zen. "The more you . . . uh . . . the more you come to practice, the more you practice Zen . . . uh . . . uh . . . the more you know . . . uh . . . uh . . . the more you realize, the more you know that . . . uh . . ." And then he concluded,

"*The more you know that life is suffering.*" We were too stunned to react. SUFFERING! The more you practice Zen, the more you realize that life is suffering!

We were so horrified we didn't have time to consider what had happened. It had never occurred to us, in our pursuit of getting high, that this might actually be another religion like Catholicism or our own familial Judaism. Zen was supposed to be cool. But was it a religion like those from which we had run away? After Suzuki Roshi's pronouncement, all we could manage was getting out of the Zen center as fast as we could. I doubt we even said thank you and goodbye.

My sister and I raced back to the East Bay. We were definitely not going to discuss what had happened. But my mind kept reviewing the events. How could he seem so light and be so heavy? Was he joking? Why would anyone practice Zen if realization of suffering was increased? Was he putting us on? Suzuki Roshi had set a hook in my mind, and I couldn't remove the discomfort. I couldn't figure my way around the dilemma his comment created because he beamed so happily while he said it.

Much, much later, my Japanese Zen teacher, Fukushima Roshi, explained how a teacher could set that hook—the hook lands below your ordinary belief systems. Fukushima Roshi told me that a teacher needs to see the student's conscious *and* unconscious delusions. It is essential that the teacher's mind is vast enough to see and contain a student's delusions. Fukushima liked to use the story of Joshu (778–897) and his disciple Gonyo to illustrate how a teacher can help a student open their mind.

In this story we find the essence of the dynamic teacher-student relationship and an explanation of how Suzuki Roshi revealed and engaged my own foolish unconscious. We did not need to tell Suzuki Roshi that we wanted to get high and that we wanted to run away from suffering. He saw our conscious delusion to get high and our unconscious delusion to avoid suffering in our lives. In Fukushima Roshi's story, Gonyo Sonja brought his dilemma and his mind for Joshu to examine when he asked this question:

> "In practice, after you have thrown everything away, what do you do?" Joshu answered with a single phrase: "Throw it away!" But Gonyo didn't understand Joshu's answer, "Throw it away!" so he persisted with another question: "I have no worldly desires, so what on earth do I throw away?" Joshu replied, "Very well then, if you can't throw it away, then keep on carrying it!"

Gonyo didn't recognize his attachment to his statement of accomplishment: "I have thrown everything away." His attachment to his belief about his accomplishment was an unconscious delusion, but he couldn't see it. For Gonyo Sonja to be able to let go of the unseen attachment, Joshu, his teacher, first had to help Gonyo see it. I did not recognize my desire to escape suffering, but Suzuki Roshi saw it and planted the hook that nagged me until I saw my own unconscious desire. Clearly Suzuki Roshi had seen beneath my sister's and my explicit request for meditation instruction. He saw what was conscious and what was unconscious.

My unconscious effort to use getting high to skip out on my lifetime portion of suffering revealed itself to me about two months later. The morning after a Berkeley party, standing outside my student apartment as my boyfriend drove away in his psychedelic bus, my gaze fell on a neighboring convalescent hospital and its aged population sitting on the glass-enclosed porch. The convalescent hospital had been there all along, but my unconscious avoidance of suffering had blocked it out of my eyesight.

BOOM—it hit me without a single intervening thought. This was my journey too; this hospital could be my home one day. I suddenly realized the depth of Suzuki Roshi's prediction—both scary and true. I would suffer, and I would know I was suffering. I felt a shift under my feet, as if the river of my life was changing course. In that moment I knew that Zen practice owned my life, and I would need to follow its lead. Through Suzuki Roshi's words I began to sense the spacious awareness that formal Zen practice offered. This mind opening was like my experience of the heavenly choir. I sensed the experience of consciousness expanding. Already in my early life I had tasted the suffering to which Suzuki Roshi was pointing. Suffering was a truth, and I had been trying to run away from it. After seeing the suffering of old age and death, I woke up to my life's work. Finding this place, where the mind met vast space, was my goal. I needed to refine my search, and it looked to me that meditation practice offered a method to find this spacious mind.

When you step into the stream, you get wet. How long does it take for you to feel the water and wish to swim in it? That varies with each person. Like music or art, we each have a spiritual capacity—our own appetite. Upon meeting Suzuki Roshi, my appetite for spiritual practice, for a relationship with God or vastness, came back into focus. That longing, like a moth to the flame, became my guide. It took me several months to find my way back to Suzuki Roshi. I learned that other people would meet him and join his Zen community in a heartbeat.

While my sister and I had made that motorcycle journey to the Zen center together, our lives took different paths. She wasn't attracted to meditation, and we didn't discuss that fateful meeting with Suzuki Roshi for many years. When I phoned her on her fiftieth birthday, nearly thirty years later, she asked me, "Do you remember that guy we met in San Francisco? Was that Suzuki Roshi?"

"Yes," I answered.

"Do you remember what he said to us?" she asked tentatively.

"Yes," I said—and I waited.

"I think he was right," she whispered.

5

WHO CARES ABOUT THE BUDDHA ANYWAY?

After meeting Suzuki Roshi, Zen meditation (zazen) became my morning ritual. My relationship to zazen was strong, but I had not yet realized the importance of a connection to a Zen teacher. In Zen training, the meeting, exchange of words, and physical correction of a teacher are weighty. These meetings affect the student, the observers, and even the teacher. The Buddha's teaching does not come from books, it is passed personally from teacher to student.

As a twenty-one-year-old UC Berkeley undergraduate, I had settled into an early morning routine of zazen at the Berkeley Zen Center. I depended on meditation and my morning rituals for mental stability. I would drive my motorcycle to the Berkeley Zen Center for the 5:00 a.m. sitting. We would have two periods of meditation followed by a silent breakfast. Sometimes it would be my turn to make breakfast, but usually I just sat and did zazen. After zazen and breakfast, I would ride my motorcycle up to Lake Anza, park, remove my clothes, and swim naked across the lake and back. The lake was cold. After my swim, I was ready for my classes.

One day, instead of morning zazen, Suzuki Roshi showed up to give a talk at the Berkeley zendo. I was furious, and I remember thinking, "Who does he think he is to interrupt *my* morning zazen?" It didn't help that I thought his talk was crap. He went on and on about the Buddha and when he was born. He had chosen that topic because it was April (1968); the date must have been close to the Buddha's birthday celebration. My anger mounted as the talk proceeded.

While I fumed and squirmed, Suzuki Roshi droned on about various calendars, different countries, and when the actual date of the Buddha's birth might be: "Maybe it is in April, but it could be in March. Some think it was this day, but others say it was that day." This was the gist of the talk. It didn't help that his English was rudimentary and barely understandable. But most importantly, the topic was of no interest to me. I loved the meditation, but I could care less about the day the Buddha was born. How was the Buddha's birthday relevant to my life today?

Since I had been attending UC Berkeley at the time of the free speech movement, I thought it was my job to challenge my professors at any opportunity. Suzuki Roshi was not immune to my role as the defiant one. When he finished his talk, he invited questions. It was the moment I was waiting for. My hand shot up; the more mature Zen students hesitated modestly.

I expressed my impatience and contempt equally through content and tone—both unmistakably direct: "Who cares when the Buddha was born? Why does it matter anyway?" My fellow Zen students wanted to hide under their cushions, but in the zendo there is no place to hide. At my intensity everyone did their best to either look away or retract their heads into their shirts.

Suzuki Roshi was not flustered in the least by my impatient tone. He had been dealing with Americans and our delusions for roughly ten years. He understood that we hippies believed that we had discovered (if not invented) consciousness. He understood that our primary concern in practice was our own self-actualization. I had no interest in the Buddhist tradition and how Buddha's life and teachings had passed from him to us. I wanted transformed consciousness, and I wanted it now. Even though Suzuki Roshi had shared the truth of suffering with me, and even though I acknowledged this truth, I still wanted to bypass my suffering through meditation.

I have learned since then that while my confrontations sometimes simply reflect my impatience, they also help me to know a person. Would he shrink? Would he become abusive? My verbal intrusions were a crude method to test a person's substance. Suzuki Roshi looked me in the eye and cleared his throat. He nodded and responded slowly and clearly: "If the Buddha existed, he was a person. If he was a person, he was born. If he was born, he had a birth date. If he had a birth date, we should be able to know it. If we cannot determine his birthday, maybe he didn't exist. If the Buddha did not exist, then why are you sitting here right now?"

I was stunned and awakened in one fell swoop. Besides the deepest meaning of his answer, I saw I was in the presence of a teacher who would not be frightened by my pointed challenges. He was not intimidated by my angry tone, and he didn't reciprocate with a put-down. I felt safe and genuinely interested in his teaching. What sustained his poise under fire? Could I rely on his composure to help me find my way through Zen practice?

I marveled at the spiritual depth of his answer. He had united my challenge, his talk, Zen practice, and that moment into one quiet thunderclap. Why indeed was I sitting zazen that early spring morning? I had thought I was sitting there because I had found this "thing" that addressed my agitated mind, a thing that allowed me to have a clearer view or that would get rid of my suffering even if it would not get me high.

But, in fact, I was also sitting there actualizing the Buddha's teaching. I now understood that, like my connection to all beings, Buddha and I had a tangible relationship. My mind and the context of Zen practice expanded.

I wondered if his whole awkward morning talk had been a setup. Was I the reactive patsy that gave him a chance to offer his deep teachings? Later I learned of his love for the image of a frog, quietly and alertly awaiting his prey—the passing fly. Was I that fly? Did he know us well enough to provoke a fly to leap forward into his waiting pounce?

The small sangha gathered that morning at the Berkeley Zen Center responded to his answer as well. Everyone was uplifted, and I escaped being scapegoated for my rudeness. In Zen training, the interaction between teacher and student is profound. Everyone who witnesses the moment and the meeting is affected. I am reminded of so many meetings recorded throughout the history of Zen. Most of all, I am reminded of Thich Nhat Hanh's teaching on how these moments open the community's heart.

> It is probable that the next Buddha will not take the form of an individual. The next Buddha may take the form of a community, a community practicing understanding and loving kindness, a community practicing mindful living. This may be the most important thing we can do for the survival of the earth.

In these practice-community exchanges, you show yourself just as you are, and in return you may be shown your place in the practice—warts and all. It won't do you any good to hide your faults and to try to look virtuous. Did you come to a learning opportunity to hide or to learn about yourself? When you have a chance to be seen, will you pretend to be without blame or will you allow yourself to be helped? It is up to the teacher to teach you both sides—an actual practice in this moment demonstrating wisdom and *your* place in the practice. You belong here, and the here includes the entire universe.

Suzuki Roshi was known for understanding this combination of acceptance and correction. He encouraged his students to show themselves rather than trying to hide difficulties. He invited students to show themselves in their questions so that he could see them. Again, Meister Eckhart's teaching: the eye with which you see God is the same eye in which you are seen. The teacher's eye and view may open a vast space. I had not yet learned to hide my flaws or talk the party line when I confronted him that morning in the Berkeley zendo. Even though I embarrassed the community, he saw me, and he moved my mind to practicing with him in the moment. The community could learn how to do this as well. He would teach, "You are all perfect just as you are, and everyone can use a little improvement." He was walking his talk and manifesting one of his favorite teachings for the community—both sides of being human Buddhas in this moment.

6

TORN PANTIES ON THE
ELECTRIC METER

Besides doing Zen meditation in Berkeley, I was living a social experiment—riding a motorcycle, living on my own, and trying to be true to my ideals. As a result of my Zen training, I was beginning to consider the weight and import of each moment. I was faced with decisions about war, poverty, and racism. Through practicing Zen, I could see that my life was formed by my presence in each moment. I wondered about which efforts mattered. How would I know what mattered?

In my last year at UC Berkeley (1967–68), I was twenty-one and living in what was known to be a dangerous part of town with the presence of drug dealers and gangs. I lived with another woman in a two-bedroom apartment with a yellow-painted kitchen floor. As UC Berkeley students, I felt that we stood out. Cognizant of our surroundings, we were both careful about our comings and goings, and I didn't go out in the neighborhood after dark. But I did go to the Berkeley Zen Center on my motorcycle for meditation every morning.

Daily group meditation and silent breakfast were affecting me. As I followed my breath, I was becoming aware of the meaning in each breath and in each moment, and the choice I had to be fully present in each moment. I was particularly affected by Suzuki Roshi's question: "If the Buddha didn't exist, what are you doing sitting here today?" I came to understand that each moment mattered—that life was a series of momentary actions that both brought us to our present circumstances and formed the quality of our lives.

One morning, after meditation at the Zen center, a woman my age described being raped in her apartment. Like me, she was not living in the best part of town. She shared that her concern during the rape was how to remain calm while it happened. She used considerable effort to not scream. I puzzled over what seemed to me to be her Zen approach to rape. Should she have fought back or screamed? I didn't know the context of the situation or that I would soon need to find my own way in such a moment.

One night soon after, I was awakened by screams. It was a female voice, and the screams were chilling and terrifying. I looked at the clock. It was 12:20 a.m.—not so late. I listened for other sounds. Doors opening or closing, footsteps, or shouting back. I was listening for the sounds of her rescue. Wouldn't someone else come for her screams? But I heard nothing. My mind expanded and I thought, "This is my moment; this is the meaning of Zen." How do we connect to a moment and realize our true nature right now? I wanted to stay in bed but the urgency, the screams, and the fact of Zen wouldn't let me. I struggled for a moment with the realization and my doubts. Was there really such a thing as facing truth, as meeting this moment? My connection to Zen and the expansion of my mind in this crisis demanded that I had to know. I got up.

I turned on my bedroom light; she was still screaming. I threw on a dress over my bedclothes and put on shoes, and she was still screaming. I went to my kitchen, turned on a light, and took a small serrated knife from the drawer. As I gripped the wooden handle tightly in my right hand, she was still screaming. It was not over yet. I went down the stairs and out the front door. I followed the screams to the back alley behind my building. As I approached, I heard the sound of running feet. But she was still screaming.

When I saw her on the ground, she was still screaming. Her wild screams scared me, and she was curled up like a frightened animal. She screamed when I reached out to touch her, to pat her back and to tell her it was just me. I worked through my fear to find a calm voice to repeat "It's just me, they're gone, you're safe." She kept screaming. I needed to repeat this message several times before she was able to look up and see me there. As she stood and moved away from the wall, I saw her panties on the electric meter. Flowered cotton and lace, hanging on the metal-and-glass dial of the meter. I left them there. I didn't know if the men or boys would come back. I didn't know how much time we had.

I put my arm over her back and led her around the corner of the building to my apartment. The door was still open; the light was still on. I locked the door behind us, and we went upstairs to the kitchen with the yellow floor. In that moment I loved that yellow floor for its cheeriness and innocence. She was still shaking, but she had stopped screaming. I dropped the small knife into the sink.

I only had powdered milk, and I used it to make her warm milk to which I added honey. I hoped it was soothing. She began to speak; she said there were three young men. She thought they were friendly. She cried about the lost underwear they had torn from her body. She cried about the humiliation, but she said they had not yet hurt her. They had run away. When she was a little calmer, we called her mother. Her mother was worried; her daughter was late coming home. She told her mother she was safe. I spoke to her mother and got the home address. I called a cab.

When the cab came, I asked the driver to come up. I told him the address and asked him how much it would cost. He accepted the twelve dollars that I gave him, and he blessed me. She hugged me, and she went home to her mother. My roommate had awakened by then, but she had not heard the screams. She heard us talking in the kitchen. The screams awakened me and I was present in the moment—I tried hard to matter, even when I was scared and even if I could fail. An emergency can expand your consciousness. I also learned that night about faith. If you trust faith, your practice will deepen and your faith in your practice will increase.

Every moment matters, and it is moment by moment that we reveal our fate. With Zen Buddhism I have studied teachings about such moments. The Japanese philosopher and Buddhist scholar Shin'ichi Hisamatsu (1889–1990) said there is one essential koan in human life: When nothing will do, what will you do? If you think about the dilemma you are in, the moment has passed. But one wrong step can cost you your life. What will you do? Where do you find guidance? How do you continue to make effort?

There is a folktale about two frogs that fell—SPLASH!—into a pail that was filled halfway with fresh milk. The level of milk was too low for them to reach the top of the pail. The sides of the pail were high, steep, and slippery, and they could not climb out no matter how hard they struggled. The frogs kicked, and they swam in circles until they both became tired. The smart frog appraised their situation more quickly, and he said, "We are done for. There is no way to get out of this bucket. I am tired, and I give up." The smart frog soon drowned and died in the bucket. But the other frog was not smart enough to realize he could not get out of his situation. So he tried anyway. He kicked and he kicked and he kicked and he kicked because he couldn't figure out what else to do. Then something strange happened. The milk began to turn thicker around him. This made kicking even harder. It was harder to swim and to kick, but still the frog tried anyway. Finally, the milk turned thick enough that the frog could stand on top of it instead of sinking in. The milk had been turned into butter through all the frog's kicking, swimming, and churning. Standing on top of the butter, he jumped out.

Like the frog, I couldn't anticipate the result of my struggle. In my Zen moment, I couldn't know what was happening. I couldn't know why she was screaming or if I would be raped or killed by her assailants. I couldn't know whether following the screams would matter at all. I had one mission—to be in that moment fully to answer her cries for help.

How much of life presents with unknown outcomes? Most of our big decisions—to marry, to have children, to go to college, to take a job—require a leap into the unknown pail of milk or the screaming back alley. But even small decisions— which route to take home, which flight to book, which subway car to enter—result in surprising opportunities and difficulties. Any moment, but especially an urgent one, can open the mind, preparing you to step into the unknown. This open mind accompanies us as we kick, swim, and paddle our way through the milk. Staying present and not abandoning effort are skills developed to meet the challenge of this very moment. Meditation, prayer, or contemplation, steadily done, helps us recognize our moments. The mind opens, but what happens next? First we awaken to the vast mind in the moment. Increasing the steadiness of our awareness helps to prepare our response. This is your life, step by step. Step right up!

7

WHAT'S LOVE GOT
TO DO WITH IT?

Suzuki Roshi performed our wedding ceremony at San Francisco Zen Center. We don't often talk about love as Zen practice, but Suzuki Roshi showed me how love and compassion can manifest in an act of silence, by not correcting a mistake or by an act of omission. I became aware of Suzuki Roshi's big mind through his response to a faux pas. His compassion and caring allowed his kind response, and through his action I learned how love could also open one's mind. Or perhaps it is within the open mind that love shines. His open mind helped me to open mine and see spiritual practice as something other than "doing it right." Love and compassionate action are another way that we discover awareness in this moment. And the compassionate action makes the mind's expansion contagious. We can feel it and see our essential oneness.

In Berkeley during the '60s, "shacking up" was one of the most common forms of dating. Getting married was considered old-fashioned—and not in a good way. My future husband and I were living together as we finished our undergraduate degrees in 1968 and contemplated immigrating to Canada so he would not be drafted for the Vietnam War. I had located a yoga camp in Quebec's Laurentian Mountains, and I believed being among yogis and yoginis would help us make a smooth transition from Berkeley to Canada. Imagine my surprise when I learned from the yoga camp director that my "fiancé" and I would not be sharing a room in the Catholic province of Quebec since it was against their laws.

When I shared the news with my live-in boyfriend and future husband, Peter Schireson, he suggested that we get married to avoid the hassle. Not the most romantic proposal, but a proposal nonetheless. The two religions—Zen and Judaism— within which I had practiced were possible sources for a wedding ceremony. We had only a month before graduating from Berkeley and immigrating to Canada. We needed to be quick and decisive in planning our wedding. First we went to visit a synagogue in Berkeley, but we had neglected to call ahead to make an appointment, and it was closed. Peter, an ardent atheistic Zen enthusiast, was outraged and wondered if God had left the building unattended because He was not working after hours. I decided to call Suzuki Roshi at the Zen Buddhist temple on Bush Street in San Francisco to see if he could provide a wedding ceremony. We set an appointment.

We had two meetings with Suzuki Roshi to plan our wedding. He explained the ceremony and asked if we could sew a *rakusu*, a traditional hand-sewn lay Buddhist surplice, to prepare for taking the bodhisattva precepts as part of the wedding ceremony. We explained that we did not have much time because we needed to leave the United States immediately following university graduation or Peter would be drafted. Suzuki Roshi nodded his understanding and agreed to do the Buddhist wedding's precepts ceremony without the traditional rakusu. Years later I learned of his sad experiences during World War II in Japan. I saw the photos of him when the Japanese army came to melt his temple bell to make more weapons. Suzuki

Roshi had lived through many experiences that made him sympathetic to our circumstances.

On the day of the wedding, I dressed in the customary "something old, something new, something borrowed, something blue" for good luck. Of the new, I wore white *tabi*, split-toe Japanese socks (that I thought were slippers) I had bought in Japantown while visiting Suzuki Roshi's Zen temple. At our preparatory meetings, I had observed Suzuki Roshi wearing tabi inside the temple. When we arrived at the temple for the wedding, Suzuki Roshi was waiting for us, watching from the front door as I exited the car wearing only the white tabi as shoes on the street, crossed Bush Street in the white tabi, climbed the stairs to the temple in my now heavily soiled white tabi, and entered the zendo still wearing my now filthy white tabi.

One does not wear street shoes into the zendo; there is an emphasis on cleanliness and purity in the Buddha Hall. If tabi are worn outside, they are worn with additional shoes covering them—shoes that are left on the shoe rack before entering the zendo. Suzuki Roshi had taught this to all his students—but I hadn't yet caught on. I didn't learn this during my wedding because he said nothing about my faux pas before, during, or after I wore dirty tabi into the zendo on that special day.

Why did Suzuki Roshi let me dirty the zendo in that way? Many years later, I reflected on my mistake. Suzuki Roshi was practicing compassion in the moment. Had any of his students been there, I am sure they would have corrected me and my dirty tabi might not have made it into the zendo. There are many sensible reasons for making sure we don't bring dirt into the zendo. At the same time, it sometimes seems that the smallest mistakes are pounced on in Zen centers. Zen centers can feel like correction machines. Mine was a not-so-small, correctable mistake.

Suzuki Roshi's choice not to correct me reminds me of a wonderful Zen folk story from China: "Why Did the Old Lady Burn Down the Hut?"

There was an old woman in China who had supported a monk for over twenty years. She had built a little hut for him and fed him while he was meditating. Finally she wondered just what progress he had made in all this time.

To find out, she obtained the help of a girl rich in desire. "Go and embrace him," she told her, "and then ask him suddenly, 'What now?'"

The girl called upon the monk and without much ado caressed him, asking him what he was going to do about it.

"An old tree grows on a cold rock in winter," replied the monk somewhat poetically. "Nowhere is there any warmth."

The girl returned and related what he had said.

"To think I fed that fellow for twenty years!" exclaimed the old woman in anger. "He showed no consideration for your needs, no disposition to explain your condition. He need not have responded to passion, but at least he should have evidenced some compassion."

She at once went to the hut of the monk and burned it down.

The old woman's monk ignored the young woman's feelings in favor of the precept to maintain celibacy. How self-centered was he to imagine that this "girl rich in desire" found him attractive? Not only did he fail to detect the ruse, but he did not question the girl's motivation or bother to explain his reluctance. If she really did want to have sex with this old monk, why didn't he question her motivation? Where was his compassion in that moment? Was he really developing his awareness of others, not just himself, through his practice in her hut? The old woman could not support the practice of a monk who spent years following rules but not learning to care for another person.

There are good reasons to follow rules and restrictions in Zen: protecting young students from manipulation and abuse, maintaining hygiene, strengthening concentration, embodying ritual, finding oneness within the group through unified activity, handling precious objects with attention, and many more. But blind obedience to rules isn't on the list as an essential part of Zen training. Clearly Suzuki Roshi was not suffering from the rule rigidity that blossoms in some Zen centers.

I was violating all the rules of protocol and hygiene by wearing street-filthy tabi into the zendo, but Suzuki Roshi would not inflict an embarrassing correction on a young bride. I believe that through his big mind, he silently surveyed the situation, did the calculations of how he might speak to me, and finally concluded that we would all survive my dirty tabi but that I might suffer from his correction. A mind opening to the entirety of circumstances concluded that saying nothing was the best course of action in this moment. While we would survive my dirty mistake, how would I remember my wedding ceremony if he had corrected me?

I remember Suzuki Roshi's response to a young woman confessing her attraction to him. He didn't answer with the "withered tree," or "I don't find you attractive," or even "I'm married and I'm a priest and I must keep my vows." He told her, "Don't worry. I have enough discipline for both of us." Just as he had left my self-esteem intact on my wedding day, through his open and compassionate mind he delivered a tender message to this young woman. Letting her retain her sense of being attractive, he told her that her desire demanded his discipline. His discipline was sufficient to take care of both of them. Importantly, she could explore her feelings safely within his integrity.

We learn here how practice may open the heart or harden it. Does the practice group focus on Buddhist principles and observing rules, or does it build a connected human bridge, out of kindness, to help students cross over to find Buddha right here and now? Some groups may focus on correct posture or correct spacing in the *kinhin* (walking meditation) line. While the formal practice helps shape the mind, is it the essential? As teachers, parents, friends, or observers, it is essential that we express the same flexible mind and love to newcomers who show up at our well-regulated training centers, to travelers from other centers, and to the many lay practitioners who are seeking meaning but not orthodoxy. I teach my own students, "You are not training to become a doormat or to treat other students as doormats." How do we practice with both full attention and open hearts? Caring for all beings requires a lot of love, and Suzuki Roshi taught me that Zen is nothing without love. The opening of mind facilitates this loving response, and it is contagious.

Part Two

Returning to the Source

The Value of Tradition

There are many ways to increase skills—attending classes; working with a mentor, guide, or coach. I was working to amplify my awareness, but all of us make choices to amplify skills. If you have practiced sports, language, or religion with a group, you may have noticed how your awareness opens and deepens—even without making eye contact or exchanging words. There are many ways we absorb a teaching—verbally and nonverbally. To amplify skills, we find the context in which to exercise those skills.

Teacher-led group settings are the recommended context for developing awareness. Throughout Zen history, the importance of finding a teacher and community has been emphasized. Attention turned on, verbal input and output reduced—our sensory awareness is stronger, more vivid. When people are angry, we can feel it. When people are joyous, we can feel that. When people are concentrating, we feel it. When we meditate, we generate a different kind of energy, and we can feel that too.

When we meditate with other people, our own ability to be present and concentrate is amplified by the energy of those around us. It is like dolphins swimming together in their pods;

their swimming movement creates water currents that may be used to lift their young or wounded. Dolphins swimming in groups can amplify their functioning as they lift each other up. Group practice—meditating or praying in a designated orderly setting, with others who are sincerely present and concentrating—lifts us up. It lights up the mind and amplifies awareness. This is a unique opportunity and benefit of group practice. When we do our practice together, it benefits all of us.

Being together is one way that awareness is amplified. Spiritual exercises, chanting, prayer, and meditation are other ways to amplify awareness. Studying the history of how a practice or training evolved is a support, but insufficient by itself to deepen practice.

But how we aim spiritual practice is essential to this process. How do we use practice effort to amplify awareness without making a specific demand? For example, in a sport, we do not demand that our feet run faster. Instead, we strengthen the muscles and technique that are used to run. To amplify awareness, we throw ourselves into the process of prayer or meditation without a demand for improvement. We develop discipline in our practice itself, not in the demand for a good outcome.

Hongzhi (1091–1157), Dogen's Chinese Dharma uncle, describes the necessary conditions for amplifying the light in his essay "With Total Trust Roam and Play in Samadhi": "Empty and desireless, cold and thin, simple and genuine, this is how to strike down and fold up the remaining habits of many lives. When the stains from old habits are exhausted, the original light appears, blazing through your skull, not admitting other matters."

In this passage, Hongzhi describes the light appearing and blazing only after the discipline has been applied to old habits of mind. We can translate his advice to very rigorous practice conditions—conditions appropriate to our age and culture—

that we hope to create during *sesshin* (intensive meditation retreat with a group). Note that he says "empty and desireless, cold and thin, simple and genuine." He does not say "satiated and still craving, fat and sassy, complicated and duplicitous."

Hongzhi places an emphasis on letting go, facing hardships nakedly without props, and taking complete responsibility for our own awareness. In group practice, we try to exchange our usual tendencies, cravings, need to be right, and special requirements for simply following the practice. We do not do what we want to do or what we feel like doing. We do not engage in the complex "he said, she said," intending to put a stop to the noncooperating factors in our lives. We allow ourselves to be forlorn and hungry, tired and irritable, solely motivated to follow the schedule without our usual litany of selfish insistence on getting our way. This is part of the process of loosening the grip of our selfish demands to allow more intimate contact with a larger Self—the Self that is universally aware.

I am very sorry to report that we have had few verified accounts of enlightenment experiences resulting from sitting in a hot tub, gazing at the moon while sipping wine. In most everyday life we are "comfort-seeking missiles." We are driven forward through an often mindless pursuit of relief from suffering or just relief from biological states of discomfort. Hence Hongzhi's admonition to be "empty and desireless, cold and thin, simple and genuine"—just get down to basics so you can heighten single-mindedness. The energy and intention of awareness become well-focused on the object of meditation. The feeling is one of letting go of desire and self-soothing comfort in pursuit of truth. This process amplifies the light of awareness.

All exercises to amplify experience and skill, whether sports or spiritual practice, help us gain confidence in being fully present. The contemporary Zen teacher Kosho Uchi-yama Roshi calls this amplification "settling the Self on the self." Which context do we choose to develop our intention? How are we guided to a deeper discipline—should we study contemporary practices or seek traditional methods? After immersing myself in contemporary practice that was based on Japanese tradition, I decided to experience the discipline and discomfort of Zen practice in Japan. Adding the cultural difficulties—language challenges, stricter patriarchal traditions, and digestive trials—was a way to take up this discipline to strengthen my awareness. I found myself frightened, cold, and challenged in traditional Japanese monasteries. Now what would I do?

8

Too Much *Mu*

The Zen *Mu* koan, created by Zen Master Joshu, is deceptively simple:

> A monk asked Joshu, "Does a dog have Buddha-nature or not?"
> Joshu answered the monk, "Mu."

According to my teacher, Keido Fukushima Roshi, this koan earned Zen Master Joshu the loving title "Joshu, you SOB." On a Rinzai Zen priests' pilgrimage to Joshu's original Chinese temple, one priest wailed "Joshu, you SOB" at the memorial site. Fukushima Roshi explained that Joshu earned the SOB by creating the Mu koan. Every Rinzai Zen priest must face down the inscrutable Mu koan as a rite of passage.

Fukushima Roshi explained the Mu koan to me this way: "When Joshu answered Mu, he expressed his Buddha-nature. When you express your Buddha-nature, what is it? Become Mu!" When I met Fukushima Roshi, I sensed his powerful Mu, but what was my Mu? Becoming Mu, becoming my essential self, was becoming the Self that precedes the mind's divisions. Rather than an abstract absence of something, Mu is a vibrant, dynamic, thrilling life force. The task was for me to find *my* Mu.

In my Western Soto Zen practice, breath was the object of my meditation. In Rinzai Zen, Mu was the object of meditation, and I trusted that Mu itself was my essential nature. During meditation with Fukushima Roshi at Tofukuji temple, I proceeded to pour my busy, thinking mind down the cracks between the slate tiles in the zendo floor. I needed a place to get rid of my mental "stuff." I aimed to become Mu without really knowing what was happening, and from time to time, I realized I had changed. For example, during one intense experience of becoming Mu, I discovered that I had become freed of language and self-reference. I came upon this realization when I left the temple during a retreat to take a bath. Otherwise I would not have known what Mu was doing with me. It's fair to say that the bath experience turned out to be a classic case of too much Mu.

Tofukuji, like the Western Zen monastery Tassajara, allows women practitioners, but not men, to bathe during sesshin. This custom was also begun at Tassajara monastery in California during the '60s when Eiheiji monastery teacher Tatsugami Roshi visited. He proclaimed, "Women smell like fish when they don't shower for a few days." God (or Buddha) forbid that women's fishy vaginal odor, real or imagined, could seep into the Zen monastery! Knowing of this Japanese belief that women's privates smelled like fish, I ate my contraband tinned tuna in the women's bathroom when I practiced in Japan. But that's a different story.

To get my bath during Tofukuji sesshin, I raced in my Zen robes down the small streets neighboring the monastery on my dinner break between periods of zazen. I didn't want to be late for the next meditation session. I rushed into the local neighborhood public bath. I'd used public baths in Japan before and mastered enough conversational Japanese to make my way around Kyoto. I had no concerns about the venture

I'd undertaken. I had, however, failed to take the power of becoming Mu into consideration.

The bathhouse attendant immediately recognized a Tofukuji monk when she saw one. In my robes, with a shaved head, no makeup, and my five-feet-ten American height, I was to her unquestionably a Western man practicing at the local temple. She took my money and waved me over to the men's side of the bathhouse. I entered the men's changing room. When I saw the roomful of naked men, I knew something was wrong. I just couldn't figure out the precise problem.

Becoming Mu, going beyond conceptual thought, putting all my mental constructions between the floor tiles, had erased my ability to identify man and woman. The concept of gender eluded me, but a hazy memory warned me that something about this bath situation was amiss. I returned to the bath lady, a question circling in my mind, but I was unable to form words. I had forgotten how to speak—not a problem during a silent Zen retreat but awkward under the circumstances. Not a single word would come out of my mouth. The bathhouse monitor figured I was a Western man without any Japanese language, so with an impatient wave of her hand she simply directed me back to the men's bath again. The second time was the charm: I grasped the problem straightaway as the naked men, all of whom had begun to eye me with suspicion, looked me over. Without a word, I exited to face the bath lady squarely.

Even though I remained speechless, the problem now showed itself on my face. She took a closer look at me. "*Onna desu ka?*" (Are *you* a woman?), she asked in a shocked voice. Still wordless, I nodded a vigorous yes! She motioned me over to the women's side of the bath, following me in to ensure that I had the requisite body parts to join the bathing women. As I undressed, she told the other women what had happened. There was much laughter and a little nervousness as I took off all my clothes. *"Ah soo desu ka,"* they all agreed, *"sugoi ama-san!"* (Wow, this is indeed one awesome [huge] nun!) I laughed along with them, completed my bath, and smiled when, days later, I heard them on the streets of the neighborhood refer to the *"sugoi ama-san"* as I passed. Thanks to becoming Mu, I had been publicly humiliated. Also thanks to becoming Mu, I experienced no residue of embarrassment or self-consciousness. Clearly there can be too much Mu to take out in public without supervision, and Mu can take the blame.

Was the teasing I experienced in the bathhouse and neighborhood a sign of intimacy or ridicule? I could never decipher whether the giggling and pet name (*Sugoi Ama-san*) were at my expense, in good fun, or both. I had experienced a lessening of self-importance. Was it Mu or my own vulnerability? I have learned it is not important to analyze the source of the lesson; it is not important to know how the lesson did its work. It is indeed wonderful to notice when we have dropped a layer of status seeking and we can just be seen as we are by ourselves and others.

9

WITBOW AND THE
GIANT BEETLE

I practiced Zen in Japan as a guest at an all-male temple. It
was usual for young men to practice under rough conditions,
less so for women. In fact, Japanese women were not allowed
to practice at Tofukuji at all—only Western women could join
the seven-day intensive Zen retreats.

I became a student of Keido Fukushima Roshi after hearing his name a third time while sitting in a public bath. I was
fifty years old and had decided to visit Japan to experience
traditional practice. I was told, while soaking, that Fukushima
Roshi was one of Kyoto's spiritual resources. Fukushima Roshi
had made regular trips to American universities and issued invitations to both college-age men and women. On one occasion,
a young woman appeared at their doorstep; she had accepted
Roshi's invitation at her college: "Come to my temple for the
shortcut to enlightenment."

At the time of her arrival, I was staying down the street at
my usual inn, Takeya Ryokan. I had found the inn when looking for a way to continue practicing at Tofukuji while honoring
my digestive challenges. When I explained to Fukushima Roshi
that I did not do well with soy, rice, or wheat, he told me that
it was impossible for me to eat the food presented at Tofukuji

during the seven-day Zen retreats. Even so, Fukushima Roshi encouraged me "to find a way to eat" so I could continue practice at the temple. I was deeply moved by his compassion and heartened by his desire that I continue to work with him. So I wandered the neighborhood asking women where I might find a place to stay near the temple. They pointed me toward Takeya, and I stayed there whenever I practiced at Tofukuji.

I had just finished a Tofukuji sesshin, seven days of intense practice at the monastery. I had continued staying at Takeya in Kyoto to give myself time to recover, practice at a more moderate pace, visit friends, shop, and sightsee. The temple administration knew where I was staying, and they called Takeya asking to speak to me. A young woman claiming to know me had arrived at the temple. She needed a place to stay and instructions in temple etiquette. Would I come over to meet with her and the temple staff? *"Kashikomarimashita,"* I answered—the old-fashioned Japanese equivalent of *HUA* (heard, understood, acknowledged) and obeying with a bow.

It turned out that I did know this woman. She was young and appealing, and seeing her at the temple, and watching the monks' gawky flirtations, brought out my protective instinct both for her and for Western Zen. I wanted to communicate through my actions that Western Zen had standards for appropriate relationships and that we would uphold them even while practicing in Japan. I secured her a room at the Takeya inn, and as a signal to the young monks, I proceeded to come to the temple to chaperone her walk home every evening she was practicing. My supervising her evening return from the temple to the inn formally ruled out the possibility of night wanderings and hanky-panky. Since the temple staff witnessed my nightly stopovers, they tracked my whereabouts as well as hers.

Thus it happened that we were both invited to celebrate a ceremony at 5:00 a.m. one morning. Groggy and still exhausted from my weeklong sesshin the week before, 3:00 a.m. to 10:00 p.m. each day, I accompanied the young woman in my formal Zen robes to the temple for the special ritual. She and I lined up on one side of the room; the monks faced us in two rows across the room. In the middle was empty tatami space.

I did my best to follow the Japanese chanting, which proceeds briskly and sounds like a roaring freight train. As we chanted, I noticed a dark object moving along the tatami in the monks' area. It was just beginning to traverse the tatami headed in our direction. I was not particularly alarmed or squeamish when it came to critters and pets. It was the size of a small black cat. As I kept my eye on the moving black thing, I noticed that it didn't walk like any cat I had seen. Cats tend to dart here and there, always concerned with finding hiding places. This thing moved boldly and deliberately. "Hmm," I mused, "it seems to be moving toward us."

When the thing sprouted wings, my alarm bells went off. As it unfolded its shiny wings, I got scared. "What the hell?" I thought to myself. "A bat in the zendo?" No, I soon discovered it was a cat-sized gigantic beetle. "Oh my," I thought—chanting all the while—"as long as it stays on the monks' side of the room, this too shall pass." I seriously considered whether prayer could work to keep it on the monks' side. It didn't work, not right then. On the contrary, my silent prayers and chanted sutras seemed to attract it straight toward me. Beetlezilla soon crossed that invisible middle line dividing us from the monks' side of the room; with a gross fluttering it was coming my way. At some point it started using the wings it had sprouted, and I heard a sickening buzz.

I have many times taught the expression "wishing it to be otherwise," or WITBOW, as a root cause of suffering. Reality presents itself, and resisting reality is not a useful solution. First we need to acknowledge reality, bow to it, and consider the current possibilities and actions. Trying to argue with reality and insist that "This isn't happening" or "I don't want this to happen" is tempting. However, resistance does not usually yield an escape—not from uncomfortable social encounters or from a gigantic sci-fi flying beetle. Reality was buzzing straight for me.

I had been trained to keep my seat, to stay in the moment, as a way to amplify awareness. While I wanted to run from the room and away from the impending gargantuan Beetle-zilla, I did not want to disgrace Western Zen—especially the female lineage. I took several breaths and chanted loudly, but it seemed as if I was just succeeding in further attracting the beetle to come my way. I also had to consider the precept of not killing, never mind the kind of mess a squished cat-sized beetle would leave on the tatami. Without a baseball bat or a giant can of insect killer, I stayed at my seat and turned to the wisdom of my Zen ancestors. What choice did I have in this very moment? There was nothing to do but be present. "Listen, Zen ancestors," I called out in my mind, "have you got any help for me?" Wishing it to be otherwise was not going to help as I squared off with Beetlezilla. What would offer protection? Who do we turn toward when we are really in trouble? Is there somewhere to aim prayers? Is there a way to make the situation larger so there is a view that will help? Staying paralyzed with fear won't help. How do we call forth resources that will help?

Turning to my Zen ancestors, I remembered that, like them, I always carried a *zagu* (bowing cloth) when wearing my formal (*okesa*) robes. The stated purpose of the zagu—folded, wrapped over the left wrist, and placed under the sleeve—was to not allow the formal robe to touch the ground while bowing. This was a reminder of the spiritual purity and power of the monk's robe. Ritual can also serve to amplify awareness. The robe was a symbol of the vow to help all beings. But in

Japanese monasteries, I witnessed older priests engaging the zagu as a prop—a cushion under the leg—during long ceremonies. Since the zagu was hidden under the large sleeve of a priest's robe, it could surreptitiously enter a ceremony room where cushions and other supports were forbidden. The zagu was an all-purpose tool that traveled at the ready, folded on the priest's wrist.

Supported by my ancestral resources, I unfurled and raised the zagu—just as a matador would use his cape to fend off a bull. Beetlezilla flew right into my zagu, as I called forth the ancestors' succor. Encountering the zagu, Beetlezilla rerouted himself toward the open doors. The monks were quietly astounded by several aspects of my behavior: my skill as a matador, my quick twirl of the zagu, and my animated behavior in the midst of a formal ceremony. I had gone beyond my reflexive WITBOW, fortified with the woven zagu wisdom of my Zen ancestors. Later, in my own private ceremony, I offered grateful prayers with incense to my ancestors for their far-reaching, ever-present wisdom.

I have come to understand WITBOW as perhaps the single greatest source of self-created suffering. When we wish something to be other than it is, we have at least three courses of action. First, we can take immediate reflexive action to stop it; because this action is immediate and reflexive, it is not well thought out. Second, we can think about how wrong this current case of WITBOW is, how it shouldn't be occurring, whose fault it is, and how unfair it is to us that this is happening. This line of WITBOW puts the focus on our unfortunate victimhood. Self-pity and self-blame don't solve much.

Or third, we can take constructive action with WITBOW. Taking a step back for perspective, we recognize that we had envisioned a different outcome. What we planned did not occur as we had planned it. But which is true—our plan for how things should turn out or the actual reality that is unfolding? In this way, we can see our expectation—our belief that things will happen the way we planned them. When we put our mistaken view back into this equation, we can begin to make space for what is actually happening. We can review our plans and how our assumptions misled us. When we have considered what didn't work, perhaps then we can turn toward a source of inspiration to provide the resources we need to cope with WITBOW.

The training I was receiving in Japan amplified my awareness and my options in that moment. I was learning the importance of keeping my seat, not disturbing others with unnecessary noise, and fully facing reality in this moment. I had also become aware of the subtle energies of spiritual ancestors who had given their lives for the continuation of the practice. It seemed to me that awareness practice was serving me well.

10

LOSING AND FINDING MY *KI*

An International Incident

I am an unlikely candidate for Zen monastic life. Besides the fact that I began monastic training in Japan at age fifty, my digestive health made it impossible for me to eat any of the foods that were standard Zen monastic cuisine. Rice was out; tofu was out; potatoes, wheat, and noodles were out. Even the tea served at Tofukuji seemed to upset my stomach. The tea problem was probably a lack of cleanliness (cup washing may have seemed unnecessary to the monks), but the rest of the restrictions grew out of my long-term digestive problems. I wasn't sure how Fukushima Roshi would respond to my special needs. My American teacher was certain that if I only practiced harder, I could overcome my food intolerances. I had tactfully *not* pointed out to him that his sincere practice had not prevented his need for several surgeries.

In 1236, Tofukuji temple, established for the Zen teacher Enni Ben'en, was the first Kyoto temple built for the express purpose of Zen practice. The temple's name comes from *To* of Todaiji (the big Buddhist temple in Nara) and *Fuku* of Ko-fukuji. At my first Tofukuji retreat, I tried to hide my physical and digestive limitations in order to gain entry to the temple and access to the koan practice with Fukushima Roshi. The cover-up worked, with big stomachaches, since it was May and the overall conditions were at least endurable, even though terribly unpleasant. However, when I came back in the winter there was an open window behind me, snow on my shoulders, and I had a broken tooth from biting a frozen energy bar stored at "room temperature" in my sleeping quarters.

One night, in response to the temperature challenges and my own physical limitations, I fainted on the meditation platform. It is not easy to faint when already seated cross-legged on the cushion, but I did it! I felt my vision starting to go black, I felt nauseated, and I knew what was coming. I positioned myself to fall backward by leaning back, with elbows behind me. My thinking: much better to fall backward onto the tatami mats than forward onto the stone floor. It was a good decision. I passed out, but I awakened feeling refreshed, with attendant monks standing over me and demanding in Japanese, *"Daijoobu desu ka?"* (Are you all right?). I nodded and hurried out to use the bathroom and splash water on my face, and to look up the Japanese words for "I fainted." These words had been missing from my vocabulary list because I hadn't needed them, but there is always a first time.

The Japanese phrase for fainting is *ki ga ushinaimashita*, or in English, I lost my *ki*. Some English speakers know the Chinese equivalent word *chi* or *qi*. Ki refers to an essential energy that is part of all living entities. In short, it can be translated as "life force." While life force can be thought of as breath or energy, it can also refer to something subtler or even more mystical. Asian martial arts and traditional Chinese medicine aim to cultivate and balance the life force. Fainting is not a loss of breath but a brief fall from participation in life. We've lost the connection to our place.

Learning the Japanese expression for fainting led me to consider the meaning of ki. What does life force mean to us?

Can we come to know it? Perhaps ki aims to guide me to sense its resonance and use it as an internal compass. What does ki feel like in the body? For me, when I rely on "gut feel," a sense of wisdom beyond thinking or verbal explanation, I am asking ki to reveal itself to me, to guide me in that moment. I have learned what the wisdom of life force feels like in my body. Feeling ki is another way that we are aware, another amplification of awareness.

Let's return to that particular temporary loss of ki—fainting on my cushion. After splashing cold water on my face and drinking some water, I learned and practiced the Japanese phrase for fainting. Watching the clock, I knew it was time to start another period of meditation back in the deep-freeze meditation hall. I headed back to my meditation cushion in the zendo to face the worried attendants. *"Ki ga ushinaimashita,"* I announced, but the monk attendants were still puzzled. *"Doshite?"* "Why?" they asked me and each other, still puzzling over what could have been a serious international incident—foreign woman dying in zazen. I did not have the vocabulary to describe low blood pressure in Japanese, so I just nodded and returned to my meditation.

With my ki regained, I knew what to do. After all, I rode horseback. When you fall off your horse, you get back on (if physically able) as soon as possible. You aim your ki at continuing, despite setbacks. You don't wait to develop fear or reasons to avoid the situation that just threw you to the ground. In life's endeavors, continuing your efforts—even after failures—determines the outcome. No one can avoid setbacks in life, but how you respond to the setbacks shapes your life. I got back on my cushion and resumed meditating. My strengthened awareness also strengthened my ki. I remember that Roshi was particularly kind to me that night when I faced him in private interview (*dokusan*).

From where did my determination to continue practice arise? I was inspired by the history of women who had practiced under terrible conditions. In particular, memory of Miaozong, a bright and bold nun from the eleventh century, touched me deeply and fed my determination to practice for the sake of women who might be denied opportunity or respect. Miaozong practiced at the Chinese temple Ching-shan. I had learned that Tofukuji, where I was practicing, was built in the image of Ching-shan—the Japanese had obtained the schematics before building Tofukuji.

Ching-shan's teacher, Dahui—a Zen ancestor to my teacher at Tofukuji, Fukushima Roshi—rejected traditional Buddhist and Confucian customs and allowed women to practice within his monastery. The women stayed in the abbot's quarters of the monastery. Following in Dahui's footsteps, Fukushima Roshi allowed Western women to stay in the abbot's quarters of Tofukuji. I had studied Miaozong's teachings before coming to Tofukuji and recognized our common connection. I felt my kinship with Miaozong, and it strengthened my resolve.

As I recount in my book *Zen Women*, while Miaozong was practicing at Ching-shan, one of Dahui's senior students, Wanan, was upset by a woman's presence—her presence—in the monastery. After reasoning with Wanan, Dahui suggested that the senior monk confront Miaozong with his concerns. Wanan went to her quarters to have that discussion. She was in her room. He called out to her, requesting an interview. Miaozong answered the monk with a question: "Is this to be a Dharma interview or a personal interview?" Wanan confirmed that this was to be a Dharma interview. Miaozong said that she would dismiss her attendants and that he needed to dismiss his.

When Wanan entered her room, he found Miaozong naked and spread-eagle on her bed. Wanan asked, "What kind of place is this?" With great composure Miaozong replied, "This is the place where all Buddhas and ancestors enter the world." Possibly contemplating his own sexual advance, Wanan asked, "And may I enter it or not?" Her calm reply: "Horses cross, asses do not," at which she closed her legs, turned her back to him, and declared, "This Dharma interview is over." Wanan, tail between his legs, returned to report the incident to his teacher. The teacher is recorded as saying, "You cannot say the beast lacks wisdom." But I think he meant, "I told you so."

If Miaozong had not prevailed with her bold genitalia-revealing action, she may have been pressured to leave the temple. If Miaozong had not been allowed to stay in the abbot's quarters at the Ching-shan monastery, would I have been allowed to stay in the abbot's quarters at Tofukuji? Her action resonated through the centuries, not only strengthening my determination to practice at Tofukuji but also supporting my bold responses to any pressure from the monks. Like Miaozong before me, my perseverance at this temple could help or hinder women who came to practice after me. I was determined to find and use my ki to honor Miaozong and to help forge a path for women who would come later.

Hazing is a part of monastic life in Japan, and as a foreigner and a woman I had been mostly spared. There were challenges, strictness, and even a surprising shove from the head monk that I'll talk about later. But after losing my ki and subsequently finding it, I sensed a change in attitude in all the Tofukuji monks. The night I fainted, I woke up laughing in the middle of the night—such as there is a middle when you only sleep four hours. I laughed because I couldn't have planned a more culturally consistent action in the land of the samurai if I had tried. By falling off my cushion and returning to my place without a word of complaint or explanation, I had established my worthiness in an international language. I could feel the shift in attitude, as if all the monks were thinking, "Maybe she is not so strong physically, but she is giving it all she's got." Just like Miaozong, my fainting and remounting my cushion had created for them an image of female strength.

How do we aim our ki? Do we know what motivates us in life? Can we amplify and release our own life force to honor what really matters to us? While we may not make immediate changes to a difficult situation, we can never know how our determination will resonate across the centuries. It is vital that we connect with our life force to actualize our own personal contribution to the human endeavor. In this way, we actualize the Buddhist or general human vow to help all beings.

11

DON'T BOW!

Keido Fukushima Roshi's essential teaching to me was "Don't bow!" Roshi was born and died on March 1. Fukushima's birthday, and his matching death day seventy-eight years later, is also my father's birthday. I didn't know Roshi's birthday when I met him, or even when I chose him as a teacher. When I found out, his birthday shared with my father's made some kind of sense. Looking back from a child's view, even though I believed otherwise, there was nothing I could have done to save either man from his death.

Meeting Fukushima Roshi for the first time in Kyoto in 1996, after thirty years of Zen practice in the United States, was a physical experience. He knocked the wind out of me, just as my first meeting with Suzuki Roshi had done. My "roshiometer" went off the scale. I knew I would need to come back to Japan to find out why and how he had done this. I sensed his power to amplify my awareness even if I didn't understand how it worked. I prepared by studying Japanese and even sharing my house with a Japanese student. A year after I had met Fukushima Roshi, I made many trips to Japan for koan practice at Tofukuji from 1998 to 2010. At first, I would go twice a year to practice. At first, he was jovial, a bright conversationalist—even in English—and he was much in demand as a speaker in Kyoto and a strict and forceful teacher. At first, he made annual trips to speak at colleges and art museums in the United States.

One year he didn't make his annual trip, and when I visited him in Kyoto I noticed he had become disabled. He was having trouble speaking and holding himself upright. I was told he had fallen, perhaps he had suffered a stroke, but that explanation didn't match well with what I saw in our meetings. I knew the Japanese did not like to talk about illness. Eventually I learned that he had Parkinson's disease.

Parkinson's disease may proceed slowly, but in Roshi's case, he sank like a stone. I saw on my subsequent visits that he could not move or speak well. It appeared that he had difficulty swallowing, and he was confined to a wheelchair. Each visit found him more compromised physically—a steady deterioration on a steep slope. I met with him privately at Tofukuji after his illness precluded his ability to offer teachings publicly.

Fukushima Roshi was no longer able to offer koan interviews during the monthly sesshin. En-san, his Dharma successor, began supervising the Japanese monks at Tofukuji. En-san, who became Harada Roshi, did not speak English. Fukushima Roshi was meeting with his English-speaking students for koan practice only rarely. Finally, his koan interviews for his Western students were offered entirely apart from the monthly sesshin. I came to understand that my time for koan study was limited by his failing ability to speak. Without taxing him, I wanted to continue my practice with him for as long as possible. He continued to offer me private interviews whenever I was able to come to Japan. Something about just being in his presence amplified my awareness.

And so it was that I found myself standing and bowing before him on a visit to Japan after arthroscopic knee surgery, a necessary repair after thirty-five years of cross-legged seated meditation. I refer to this kind of knee problem as a sports injury or an occupational hazard. As my fainting on the cushion demonstrated, I was proud to push through difficulty. Roshi had known about my knee problem prior to my surgery. On this occasion he instructed me to take a seat without bowing. I began to bow anyway, as I mentioned the Japanese word for surgery—*shujutsu*—to tell him the knee was now suitable for bowing after receiving surgery. That is when he yelled at me—"DON'T BOW!"—with an unexpected ferocity that penetrated my brain and my stubborn pride. My mind opened; I did not bow, and we continued our dokusan.

Clearly Roshi's own compromised physical experience had affected his awareness and his teaching style. He had recognized the urgency of my self-care when it was still possible to avoid further injury. He had previously been practical about finding a way for me to continue meditating at Tofukuji—even through physical challenges. Knowing about my knee problem, he had suggested alternative sitting positions—even a stuffed ottoman. At first I tried to hide my digestive problems from him. Finally, when I explained my limitations, he understood. He told me to find a way to eat first, and to sit when I could. Clearly he understood one could not fake it as far as the body was concerned. The body keeps score. You can decide to do what your body doesn't like, but the body is the ultimate umpire.

This had not been the case with my American Zen teacher, who told me that my digestive difficulties were a result of my "practice failure." If only I practiced with less stubbornness, I would overcome my digestive problems. My American Zen teacher told me that I needed to eat the same food prepared for the other practitioners and to find a way to strengthen my intention to practice. My body was not up for this challenge. I was still finding what did and did not cause me abdominal pain. I would need to do that away from my American teacher—my body said, "He is not good for your health." In a relationship where I was blamed for my health problem, he was applying the rules mechanically to my detriment. I needed to closely study my body's relationship to food. Apparently I was not able to tell my digestive system what to do. It needed to tell me what to eat, and it did.

Fukushima Roshi's impassioned instructions regarding self-care opened my mind and became a core teaching for me and consequently for my own students. What did it mean to not bow? The teaching that I offered to my students, after Fukushima Roshi's command, was that you don't fool yourself about your own body, and you don't knowingly sacrifice your body for some imagined samurai ideal. The go-beyond-pain instructions we received from Zen's samurai tradition were not meant to deny the reality of our specific physical needs. These instructions may have helped a samurai class in Japan fight on and face their own death out of loyalty to their lord. These instructions may help a squirmy meditator practice stillness. Practice today means loyalty to developing your awareness, not blind obedience to rules from another culture or era. And by living through intimate body awareness, you can know how to take care of your body. It tells you, you do not tell it. The body's wisdom is an amplification of your awareness. Listen up!

When I practiced the Dharma transmission ceremony to become an independent Zen teacher, I learned an expression: "Save the body, it is the fruit of many lifetimes." While we can practice with physical disability, as far as we know, being alive is the only realm in which we may engage in Buddhist practice. As a living being, one only has so many breaths. How shall we use these breaths and our embodied time to practice? We can be in touch with our physical constraints to practice wisely, or we can use our practice to repress pain, look "good" on the cushion, and emphasize ableism in our practice community.

"Don't bow" has become a core teaching for me with my own students. Not bowing includes offering a guest kitchen for personal food preparation, single rooms with personal bathrooms, and flexibility of physical demands in practice to include as many differently abled practitioners as possible.

The importance of Roshi's command needs to be internalized in every meditation student. All of us need to understand for ourselves and our own bodies the teaching of "Don't bow!" While we may be reminded by a teacher or other ally to take care, we are the only ones inside our own bodies. Don't let ideas of "looking good" veto your own good sense about what your body needs. "Don't bow" means don't pretend, don't think ritual is more important than you are, don't enslave yourself to an ideal, don't repress your own pain and especially, for God's sake, don't bow after knee surgery.

Whether or not you are on the cushion doing meditation or engaging in other physical activities, "Don't bow" is an important maxim. It is not all in your mind; there are physical issues that you cannot use the power of positive thinking to erase. Are you trying to reach a goal—for example, a six-minute mile? Do you want to go back to playing a sport from your youth? Do you want to reach a certain clothing size? Please consider your body—the fruit of many lifetimes (or even just one)—as the source of wisdom for what is best for you now. Let your body expand your awareness. Do not try to aim for or fit yourself into a number. Consider what your body needs, what is best for your health. Don't try to push your body around like an object. Instead, let your body guide you to what it needs. Don't bow!

12

THE MONK WHO HIT ME

Tofukuji is one of the *gozan* (five mountains), the five famous temples of Kyoto. The rituals for young Japanese monks in training—including beatings, hazing, jobs, and pecking order—are well established. Less well established are temple rules for Western practitioners, and not at all well known are practices for women. As far as I know, Fukushima Roshi was the first Tofukuji abbot to encourage Westerners to practice there, and the first abbot to allow Western women to practice alongside the training monks in the training hall (*sodo*).

Only a few Western women took Fukushima Roshi up on his offer to practice at the temple, and one Japanese woman who was married to an American. Women's practice occurred at the temple during a period of roughly twenty years, and since Fukushima Roshi's death in 2011, Westerners and women are no longer encouraged to attend the monthly seven-day meditation retreats. Today, one must speak Japanese in order to participate. When I was invited to attend my first weeklong retreat in 1998, I was given no instructions regarding the temple's etiquette or schedule. I had to rely on observation and do my best to follow along. If I made a big mistake, I was informed, one way or another.

One of the rituals I learned by observation was exit and entrance for koan dokusan (a private interview with the roshi). Through practice, we monks learned to be completely absorbed in our koan. Through ritual, we learned to be completely present in our physical activity. Five times a day, we were required to present our insights on our koan in private interview. Almost always, we were "rung out" by Roshi as he rang his little bell. This meant our answer was wrong. Sometimes Roshi would comment, grunt, or shake his head, but we were still wrong.

The pecking order at Tofukuji was rigid: Japanese monks from most senior to least senior, followed by other Asian monks by seniority, followed by most senior to least senior male Western Zen students (whether ordained or not), followed by Western women in order of seniority (Japanese women were not admitted to the training hall). As a Western woman, I was always last to leave the meditation hall for dokusan, last to have my private interview, and last to reenter the meditation hall for the chanting service, lunch, or tea that followed dokusan.

I learned how to hurry along, returning to the zendo without making clomping noises on the wooden floorboards. I also learned how to put on my rubber flip-flops silently and quickly before I reentered the silence of the hall. It was not an easy task, but I managed it efficiently. Imagine my surprise one day when the head monk slapped and shoved me as I reentered the meditation hall. On one hand, I understood there was never enough effort. A Zen maxim for practice is "not enough, not yet, not yet enough." On the other hand, as a victim of childhood physical abuse, and as a psychologist who counseled victims of domestic violence, I was stunned. I needed to talk to someone about this violation. I knew there was a rule; Western women, practicing at Tofukuji, were not to be hit.

When I talked to an American woman who had practiced at the temple for many years, she said, "Oh, he didn't mean anything by it." With only minimal consideration, I discounted her answer as the response of someone who had neither experienced abuse nor its consequences or of someone who was willing to tolerate abuse. Neither category applied to me. I also know the ways that bullies work. They enjoy the sense of power that allows them to hurt others with or without provocation. For a bully, asserting power or pain without provocation may feel the best.

I considered my options. I could talk to Roshi, but I felt that would create even more difficulties for me with the monks. I would become the zendo snitch. Knowing how important loyalty was in that setting, I ruled out that option. I couldn't think of anyone who could help me with this situation. My experience and psychological training had taught me that bullies who get away with bullying continue to bully the victims who allow it. I had vowed to practice for the sake of other beings; tolerating bullying would not help others who came after me.

I continued to puzzle about what to do in an environment where I was tasked with finding the essence of Self and no-Self. I thought that being hit selflessly was going too far for a Westerner. How to respond? Did it matter if "I" were hit or ignored? Did it matter whether the monk was a bully? What mattered? I was thrown back to the teachings of Rinzai. After all, he had invented this practice I was engaged in.

In *Essays in Zen Buddhism*, D. T. Suzuki quoted Rinzai as saying:

> Do not be deceived by others. Inwardly or outwardly, if you encounter any obstacles, lay them low right away. If you encounter the Buddha [as merely a mind object], slay him; if you encounter the Patriarch, slay him; if you

encounter the parent or the relative, slay them all without hesitation, for this is the only way to deliverance. Do not get yourself entangled with any object, but stand above, pass on, and be free.

Rinzai was teaching that you could not amplify awareness if you were caught by circumstances. Clearly I was caught by this event, this mind object, but how could I slay it and continue the process of amplifying my awareness? The question occupied me completely as my personal koan. Drop it or slay it, which was right? Eventually I realized that I hadn't dropped it, and I couldn't drop it. What to do? The mind object wouldn't budge from this question: "What does a feminist do to stand up for herself and other women in this abusive situation?" Like my koan work, I could not resolve the question with my thinking mind, so I turned the response over to the awareness of the body's wisdom.

I concluded that if the head monk touched me again, I would let my body decide what to do. My body was keeping score. I'd grown up with a brother and sister; I knew how to fight. If my body decided to punch the abusive monk in the face, I would let my fist express its wisdom. I didn't pack much of a punch, but he would get the idea. If he hurt me afterward, so be it. If I was thrown out of the temple for aggressive behavior, so be it. Roshi knew me, a mature grandmother, usually of sane mind. Roshi would know something had happened, and he would require a full explanation. My mind settled; my body awareness would lead the way. I had found my deliverance—trusting my body awareness to handle whatever arose.

As it happened, the head monk never touched me again, but he did attempt to bully me and correct my sitting posture. I had obtained permission from Roshi to sit in any posture that suited me since I was not officially a monk of that temple.

I was seated in a kneeling position with a cushion supporting my buttocks. From across the room, the head monk indicated with gestures that he was ordering me to go back to a cross-legged posture. I let my body answer by looking him straight in the eye and not moving my leg position. Instead, I moved my head ever so slowly, side to side, an unmistakable nonverbal no. He quickly looked away and snapped back into his own zazen posture.

He never bothered me again. I was not his passive victim to push around or bully. Customarily, the Japanese never say no. They may say *chotto* (sort of) and tilt their head to the right. This means "No damn way!" While the word for no does exist, and the head gesture can give a negative response to any question, meeting the head monk with a no is just not done. I guess if you use your body's wisdom to slay obstacles in the service of practice, the karma of yes and no takes care of itself. Wisdom can transcend the temple rules and pecking order.

There is always a way to find freedom. Your freedom may be found in becoming your Self completely or in letting go of the Self. Fukushima Roshi taught about *jiyu*, which he explained as freedom. Jiyu means relying on the self—the Self we know as me, or the Self that exists when we let go of attachment to me. Roshi emphasized that it was a different freedom than we understood in the West. He explained further: "It is not freedom *from*, it is freedom *to*." My freedom depended on relying on my connection to my own body awareness— something I could trust.

I learned that I couldn't find freedom from oppressive circumstances—not even in the zendo. I could, however, find freedom to clarify myself even in the most tightly regimented settings. We all can. First, we need to identify what we are experiencing as oppression. Once we have seen where and how we feel restricted, we can find the mind that is unafraid to stand up to or even to let go of the difficulty.

The mind and awareness can be trained to become clearer and more flexible. From that position, we can trust that a creative solution will emerge as needed. However, if we are stuck feeling oppressed or angry about the oppression, the mind is also stuck in its opinion of what happened. When we are stuck in an uncomfortable situation and we have not come to terms with it, we are stuck. We are not amplifying awareness.

Find the space to turn the mind; even a little wiggle room will help. While you can't resolve all worldly difficulties in this way, why not at least find the freedom of awareness in your mind? Clearing your mind, not sticking to insults, freeing the mind of the obstacle of righteousness, opens you up to amplified awareness and the possibility for a creative response. When you have worked through your stubbornness, your feelings of injury and anger, you can see if there is anything left to do—whether it is letting go or standing strong. With practice that amplifies awareness, you can trust your response and let it move you through difficulty.

13

DEATH BY *SEIZA*

Early in my Japanese monastic practice, I had a wonderful trip to Eiheiji, the head temple for Soto Zen in Japan. Eiheiji has the stature and grandeur of the Vatican in Rome. Its scenery, dignity, deep practice, and beautiful furnishings inspire reverie and command presence. I was visiting Eiheiji for the *shuso* ceremony for Shungo Suzuki. Shungo, the son of Hoitsu Suzuki Roshi and the grandson of Suzuki Roshi, had earned the top honorary position among the monks that year resulting in his shuso ceremony. Several busloads of *Rinso-in danka-san*, members of Suzuki's home temple, were traveling to Eiheiji for the ceremony. It was a full day's ride, which included karaoke on the bus. I distinguished myself in karaoke with my rendition of the Beatles' "Yesterday," receiving several compliments on my excellent English.

The shuso ceremony took place over the course of several days. I shared a room with Hoitsu Suzuki Roshi's wife and daughters. As they prepared for their formal appearance in kimono and traditionally styled long hair, I was astonished at their ability to breathe with hairspray so thick. Although I had to admire the architectural handiwork of their elaborate hair, as their roommate I became concerned that I would experience death by hairspray.

Another Eiheiji hazard concerned my fear of death by intestinal blockage. Every meal was rice, pickles, and unidentifiable fried rubbery stuff (most likely fried tofu). In texture, it closely resembled vulcanized rubber tire. I'm sure the meals were lavish by monastic standards, and delicious to Japanese people who seem to have evolved a genetic ability to digest vulcanized rubber tofu. I was not nearly as talented; in fact, I am intestinally challenged. I managed to survive the food challenge because of my American seatmate at the table. He was exceptionally sturdy, and he loved Japanese food. I would surreptitiously pass most of my food to him, and I could eat my dried fruit and nuts later in secret. Finally, even he had eaten enough, and he refused my offerings. At that point I had to sneak the leftovers out in my sleeve. *Mottainai*—one must never waste!—was a common expression in Zen temples.

While I was fairly certain I had avoided the first two death threats—death by intestinal blockage and death by massive hairspray inhalation—it became clear to me that I faced a bigger danger in the hours ahead. I might die—or at least be permanently paralyzed—by *seiza* posture—kneeling with hips on ankles, without a cushion, on a tatami mat. The ceremony included many uninterrupted hours of seiza. I was fifty-two years old at the time, and I had already used up most of my knee cartilage through many years of zazen seated in the lotus posture. The beauty of Eiheiji, the rituals, the early mornings, and the fears of perishing all served to amplify my awareness.

At the shuso ceremony, I was seated among the *gonin*, the honorable guests of the Suzukis. I learned a great deal from these honorable older priests. First, they had done their rigorous training as young men. Sitting meditation all day and all night was no longer required of them. And they would sneak in their zagus, their bowing cloths, in order to cushion their knees. I marveled that we had not learned in America how to protect ourselves from permanent knee damage as we aged. I guessed we missed out on "old priest" practice because the founding teacher at San Francisco Zen Center, Shunryu Suzuki Roshi, had died when we were still young. His young disciples hadn't learned how older priests coped, how to cope with aging when facing Zen's physical challenges.

Older temple priests and one temple nun, Shunko-san, were among the gonin. The nun had excellent old-age technique; she concealed a fold-up seiza bench in her very large formal robe sleeves and brought it out to use for the ceremony. A seiza bench has two wooden ends and a padded seat. The bench elevates the buttocks off the cushion, relieving pressure on knees and thighs. I could only marvel at her genius. She had anticipated the full-length horror of the seiza, and she had prepared by sneaking the small but effective seiza bench into the zendo inside her sleeve.

Soon her scheme was interrupted by an Eiheiji temple monk official who told her that he "was sure she would be more comfortable in a chair." Without the faintest hint of reluctance, and offering a formal bow of gratitude, she accepted the chair as her seat and put the bench back in her sleeve. Of course, she had known all along that the chair was an option but had chosen a more dignified seated position on the bench. I understood the embarrassment that she faced being seen seated in a chair, differently from all the other male monks. I felt her discomfort keenly since we were the only two ordained women among the hundreds of male priests. As far as we could tell, all the men were sitting in seiza, presumably ready to face their own crippling demise.

The entire history of the Zen nuns' practice weighed on me in that moment, when past, present, and future became fused. How will I express the history in this moment that nourishes the future? Specifically, I was reminded of the Buddha's refusal to allow women ordination. The nuns, whose ordination restrictions put them in a second-class order, endured humiliations and attacks throughout the centuries. And now this confrontation right before my eyes at the head temple for the Soto Zen sect. As I thought about my female Zen ancestors, I recalled the Eight Special Rules for Buddhist nuns. In particular, number 8, as worded in my book *Zen Women*, sums them up:

8. Admonition of monks by nuns is forbidden; admonition of nuns by monks is not forbidden.

Based on early Buddhist rules, nuns were under the direction of monks. The most senior nun was junior to the most junior monk. Looking at my fellow female Zen nun Shunko-san, it was clear that she was senior to this Eiheiji monk. I knew she had her own temple. The same was true of me. But our functional seniority was irrelevant in this formal Japanese setting. Sometimes the weight of twenty-five hundred years lands on one moment, intensifying attention and awareness. I couldn't argue with this junior monk on Shunko-san's behalf—according to the Buddha's teaching, he was her senior.

Again I reached deeply into my awareness and my responsibility to the nuns' order. How was I to make a statement and still be part of the ceremony without disgracing the Suzuki family? I waited until the young monk official departed and quietly asked Shunko-san if I could borrow the bench. She passed it over. As soon as I had made myself comfortable on the seiza bench, the young monk returned. He repeated his assurance that I would be much more comfortable in a chair. I did not want to sit in a chair, fearing that in the future Abbess Zenkei Blanche Hartman would see pictures of the ceremony and scold my feeble representation of Western Zen women at Eiheiji. Zenkei Blanche Hartman had been the first female abbess at San Francisco Zen Center; she was a mentor and close friend. She had inspired me, and I wanted to inspire other women to forge ahead despite the hardships. I did not want to seem less able than the monks while representing all of my female ancestors.

Unlike Shunko-san, the Japanese Soto nun, I did not report to Eiheiji temple as an American Zen nun. In fact, American Soto Zen nuns don't follow the Eight Special Rules. How could I hold my ground and stand up for the women's lineage? I looked the monk squarely in the eyes and said *"Arrigato, demo iie"* (Thank you, but no) with a genuine smile. The monk's expression changed from being in command to rapid deflation. He had probably never encountered insubordination by a woman in his formal role. He left our seating area immediately. He may have instinctively believed in the Eight Special Rules and relied on the authority of his position, but in this particular exchange he didn't have a way to enforce those rules.

I was able to sit upright, in endurable pain, on my seiza bench for the several-hours-long ceremony. I couldn't tell if I was uplifting or disgracing the women's lineage, so I sat taller. Some others seated around me experienced near-death by seiza. My rather accomplished and sturdy American male seatmate was even reduced to groaning. I had often wondered whether strong ligaments, tendons, and joints were seen as equivalent to Zen accomplishment. Do we glorify teachers who can sit seiza and full lotus—mistaking good joints and balanced musculature for spiritual accomplishment?

After the ceremony, the Suzuki family marveled at my miraculous seiza stamina and my continuing ability to walk. The family had been seated at a distance in the ceremonial hall that seated several hundred observers. I confessed my use of the bench to the Suzuki family, and we laughed together. From a distance, my use of the bench was hidden under my robes, enabling me to look stronger than I was. From a distance, maybe you couldn't tell whether I was a monk or a nun. Perhaps exposing my inability, and allowing the monks' seiza fortitude to shine in contrast, was the intended purpose of putting me and Shunko-san in chairs. Maybe, like all of women's history in Buddhism, we were being put in our place. But I have never been good at getting into that position.

Feeling the weight of twenty-five hundred years of Buddhist culture, and as the guest of a distinguished Japanese family, I found myself in a bind. I wanted to express the equality of men and women. I wanted to support Shunko-san's efforts and those of all women in this male-dominated institution. However, I knew straying too far from the protocol would have caused embarrassment to my host family. This is a feminist's dilemma—how to find your authentic place in a male-dominated environment. Do you follow the lead of women who have survived through submission? Do you risk your precious place for a single statement of equality?

We each need to find a way to fulfill our ideals and to respect some of the different values. I found it easier to make the point because Shunko-san was involved. I wanted to stand up for another who was being put down. I became a little taller and a little stronger by relying on awareness of the moment in a larger context.

What brings out your principles? How do you decide when to stand up and when to back down? Surely there are moments for each of us—moments when we want to fit in with a group but feel that something is amiss. Take your breath, settle your mind, and listen to the amplified awareness in your body. What is at stake and what are the consequences? Being embarrassed, while weighty, doesn't carry the same consequences as, say, being arrested. Choose wisely with a realistic view of consequences.

In the context of today's women's marches, it is good for us to remember that twenty-five hundred years ago, Mahapajapati, the Buddha's aunt and stepmother, led the first women's march. She stood her ground against her powerful stepson (Buddha), the leader of the religious order she wished to join. For the sake of the women she taught, she risked everything. The Buddha had cautioned her to not set her heart on women's ordination. But she persisted. She led a 150-mile march, with barefoot nun aspirants, to appeal to the Buddha for female ordination. She took a radical stance and action without which we might not have women accepted as Buddhist nuns today. I bow down to Mahapajapati, who fought for women's ordination and directly affected my own life. Her strength and courageous actions affect Buddhism across more than twenty-five hundred years. We need to remember that our decision to stand up for an ideal can matter more than we can realize in any moment.

Part Three

MAKING IT YOUR OWN
Circulating Awareness in the Body

After formal Zen practice in Japan and the United States, I returned to my local neighborhood Zen center to continue practicing with my friends and my American root teacher. I was curious to see how the effects of my strict traditional practice in Japan would affect my quick-to-anger personality. When I felt disliked or disregarded, would my easily hurt feelings continue to force me to quit interacting? Would I be able to remain calm and to speak up when facing ongoing misogyny in my local center? I had put so much effort into deepening and amplifying my awareness, how would I allow this awareness to circulate while I was interacting with friends and peers, particularly in emotional circumstances?

Of course, awareness is circulating with or without our conscious efforts. But it is good to participate. I love the scene in *To Have and Have Not* when Lauren Bacall kisses Humphrey Bogart once, then she tries again with a second kiss. Her conclusion: "It's so much better when you help." We also need to "help" the wisdom of awareness circulate throughout the body in several ways. We exercise awareness in the body by engaging in relationships in which we remain aware; being aware of emotions in the body; engaging in close relationships;

participating in writing, art or games, presentations, and culturally familiar rituals with our practice group. We may begin practicing awareness in an Asian meditation center and then expand our practice in our native language and culture. We have a stake in these activities since they belong to our relationships in our culture. In short, we really care!

We have learned many meditation practices from their traditional Asian roots, but we have also begun to modify and add our own Western ways of practice. When we practice in our own vernacular, our emotions are increasingly aroused. Many Asian Buddhists enter religious practice as infants sitting on their grandmothers' laps. They feel surrounded by love, caring, and relationship. Practitioners who adopt Buddhism as adults are missing this basic emotional fabric. Now in Western centers we are developing the sense of family, social bonds, and play that other spiritual practitioners developed within family worship.

We have developed various activities in the West to help us bond, to arouse our feelings, and to energize our creativity. These practices, translated in our Western idiom, circulate the amplified awareness. If meditating, chanting, or praying is only a solitary practice, it may become divorced from human feelings and compassion. Just contemplating your own navel, your private prayers, and your breathing, you may become stuck. You may feel fragile; you may feel that spiritual practice is the only place you are safe. You may feel baffled and disappointed when you reenter your personal life. And you may be tempted to say, "Wait a minute here, you people are not following my schedule or even basic politeness." In short, solitary practice may add to self-absorption.

For most of us, developing awareness is not the end of the task. Integrating awareness into social life—a vow to awaken with all beings—is described in Zen terms as the last stage of integrating Zen practice. While our inner life can be infinitely fascinating, the greatest benefit of spiritual practice is to benefit other people. By circulating the amplified awareness into emotional, social, and creative activity, we are brought closer to fulfilling our human purpose.

14

DARLENE'S FOOT IN THE AIR

In *Everyday Zen*, the American Zen teacher Charlotte Joko Beck describes a practice useful in working with pain and suffering so they do not take over our experience. Beck describes the process of building a bigger container in which we step back and observe what we are experiencing. Just as the salty taste diminishes when we dissolve salt in more water, so pain is less sharp when we can hold it in a larger perspective. Trying to completely tune out pain does not create a larger perspective. We dilute pain when we create more space around the experience. I learned about living with chronic and severe pain from my friend and Dharma sister Darlene Cohen.

Darlene struggled with rheumatoid arthritis (RA) for more than thirty years. She suffered pain in every joint. From her early thirties, she watched her joints twist and turn gnarly. As a girl, she had witnessed her mother suffer the same disease, and when she was attacked by RA, she felt helpless to stop it. Over the course of her illness, and up until her death in 2012, Darlene shared her remarkable ability to face pain with composure as an essential Zen teaching. When I suffered chronic knee pain, a common Zen sports injury, I spoke with her about it. She said, "Oh, yes, knee surgery; thank God we only have two knees!" When I told her about throwing my back out after wearing cute shoes, she said, "Yes, back pain: the price we pay for cute shoes." Darlene knew a few things about pain and how to live in pain with style and humor.

As a Dharma teacher, to be able to work with her students, Darlene had to balance meditation and medication. Her pain was relentless and excruciating, and she had to learn to live with it in order to keep going and continue her teaching. She told me once about how her pain had kept her from walking up the steps to the Zen center for meditation. On some days, she would walk from her apartment, look at the steps, take one step, turn around, and go home. The pain of climbing the stairs had defeated her. Zen practice was her most precious purpose, and her joint pain was stealing it from her.

Painful Zen center stairs did not make Darlene quit practice. She found ways to focus on the light moving across her room, on her own breath, on sweet moments here and there, and over time she discovered how to focus her attention on her foot in the air rather than her foot on the hard concrete step. There was bliss in that freely moving foot; she learned to bring all her attention to that blissful freedom. She moved her mind from the painful foot—the meeting of her weight and the stair's hard surface—to the foot's freedom flying through the air. This was Darlene's practice of the Foot in the Air.

Pain is compelling for a reason. Pain owns our attention in order to alert us to problems in the body; it compels us to seek solutions to keep ourselves alive. But when pain is chronic, and when we realize we can't readily resolve it, pain can drag us down. It can lead to inactivity, depression, purposelessness, and, finally, even to loss of life. We all have pain, and sooner or later we will all face its relentless demands. So how do we let go of the painful experience of the tender foot on the ground and turn the mind's eye to the Foot in the Air? This is an essential question in Zen: How do I practice with *my* suffering?

I have my own unique ability to develop joint pain in various locations. Recently I was working on a persistent shoulder pain with exercise, chiropractic therapy, acupuncture, and supplements. When it came roaring back—despite the treatments—with severely constricted movement, I sought out yet another doctor. She asked me to lift my arm. I could only do it slowly and by grabbing and lifting the arm on my injured side with my other hand. The doctor asked me if I was unable to lift my arm because of the pain, the weakness, or my anticipation of pain. I really couldn't say which it was—it was all three conditions. I realized that anticipation of pain—which is freely supplied by the body-mind equipment—was also limiting my movement.

When the body-mind anticipates pain, it slams on the brakes. The mind can act like Velcro during pain—preventing movement. How do we encourage the mind to be more slippery—like Teflon—in the face of pain? We need to bring the mind to the freedom in the body—the spaces not in pain—rather than to the pain itself. For my shoulder, I brought my mind to raising the other arm. Even though the shoulder required medical treatment, I practiced raising my two arms at the same time, and I could move the injured arm more freely. One arm was in the air, the other followed faithfully.

Learning how to work with pain is an important task. Trying to tune out pain quickly becomes an exhausting tug of war. Rather than fight it, we need to make more space for it. The secret to creating a larger perspective is to train the mind to let go of the objects of awareness and align with awareness itself. In this way, the specific object of awareness becomes background and awareness itself becomes foreground. Awareness expands, as Charlotte Joko Beck describes in the practice in *Everyday Zen* A Bigger Container:

This practice of making A Bigger Container is essentially spiritual because it is essentially nothing at all. A Bigger Container isn't a thing; awareness is not a thing; the witness is not a thing or a person. There is not somebody witnessing. Nevertheless, that which can witness my mind and body must be other than my mind and body.

Witnessing awareness is not quite a thing; it arises within the body-mind equipment. Mysteriously, the mind and body are reflected in this space of awareness. We form a connection to this awareness, which is then amplified and allows for a bigger container within which the pain has space to dissolve—just as salt dissolves more thoroughly in more water. Darlene's Foot in the Air is an example of this kind of practice. Darlene trained herself to expand and circulate her awareness to become a bigger container that included the space around the painful foot, the ground, and finally the foot flying through the air. The pain did not magically disappear. Everything was still there, but the physical pain was only part of the bigger space of awareness. Awareness contained a foot moving in the air, the air, and the painful foot on the ground. The awareness was circulating the pain into the movement in the air.

Pain grabs our attention, but how can we open the mind? When we are working with pain, with suffering, where will we focus? Which part of the experience will we underline? Where do we teach our attention to land? We can't will ourselves to forget or ignore the painful foot on the ground, and we can't demand that our attention land on the free-flying foot. First, we need to practice the art of intimacy with awareness. When we are intimate with our awareness, when we become awareness itself, we can circulate the pain within the body moving through space. The container expands naturally. Awareness ceases sticking to the pain. Instead, it softens to notice everything surrounding the pain. Attention can circulate freely.

Once, a student explained to me how he was attempting to use his meditation practice to cope with the loss of a relationship. I asked him how he was practicing with his suffering. "Actually, I bring up the teachings of emptiness, impermanence, and the truth of suffering, but none of it helps," he said sadly. His mind would consider these Buddhist concepts but then return to his pain—to find it still hurt. You can't argue yourself out of pain.

I spoke to him about Darlene's Foot in the Air practice, but he still looked puzzled. "Okay," I said, "the Foot in the Air for you is expanding your view of your pain to the space and the soft feeling of tenderness with which you can envelop the pain. Where is the space around the pain? What happens when you bring your attention to the tender space around your painful heart, not to the pain itself? What happens when you try to expand your attention, circulate the pain, and meet your pain with gentle love? That is your practice of the Foot in the Air."

You cannot will away your pain by memorizing Buddhist concepts, by trying not to feel, or by saying the pain is just empty. Communicating with your body and mind is the first step. Then let the awareness carry the pain to a bigger space. I asked my student, "How do you find the space around your painful heart when you are suffering?" Did I detect his subtle response—a welling in his eyes? Was he allowing himself to include the space around the pain so he could tolerate it? Did he loosen his grip on his loss, feel the space around his heart, and find the Foot in the Air? Can you?

15

NAKED IN THE ZENDO

Master, I Have Been Enlightened

Sitting in meditation can make one sensitive and intuitive. It can also make you self-conscious and hypervigilant about making mistakes in the zendo in front of Buddha and all those people watching. Of course, there were my ordinary mistakes such as pouring boiling water on the teacher when serving tea or dropping food when serving the community. But there are also deeply archetypal scenes that haunt dreams and day-dreams. These are imaginary and dreadful situations where you appear naked in the zendo, wet your pants, or offer loud flatulence when bowing.

I have not yet enacted one of my more dreaded embar-rassments, even though they may appear in my dreams or nightmares. I was, however, in the zendo when someone else did what I most feared—in full view of the community. Such a scene, during a meditation retreat, is embedded in the psyche and never forgotten. Wisdom is exposed for the perpetrator by living through embarrassment during a powerful enact-ment. For the observer, spiritual growth can also be firmly rooted in their path. Seeing someone live through your worst nightmare without lasting damage can be enlightening. The emotions are engaged, and they circulate awareness and embarrassment in the body.

In one seven-day sesshin at the Berkeley Zen Center, my job was to serve the food. All participants took part in organizing the retreat's activities. When the meals were ready, I helped the cook put the food in the appropriate pots and bring the food to the zendo. In the zendo, the cook started the elaborate meal ceremony by offering three full bows to the community. The cook did his bows on a cushion and brought his head all the way to the floor as a symbol of respect for the source of the food and those who would receive it. This short but poignant ritual is accompanied by bells. All attention was tuned up; hungry meditators could smell the food and were anticipating a delicious meal and a rest thereafter.

The cook for that meal, George, was a warmhearted and friendly man in his seventies. He was well versed in how to enact the ritual. He bowed once—ding. He bowed twice—ding. And he bowed a third time—ding! But something went horribly wrong; when he stood up from his third bow, his sweatpants dropped from his waist and went down to his feet. George stood briefly and bravely in his underwear, in front of Buddha and all retreatants. When he realized that his pants were no longer in place, he scooped them up, pulled them back on, and hurried out of the zendo without stopping to enjoy lunch.

My first reaction was to pretend that George's pants had not fallen off, so I could begin serving the food without further incident—let's cover up what is uncomfortable because I have a schedule to keep. But I looked up to find Sojun Roshi, seated at the front of the room, convulsed with laughter—contagious laughter. And so, I stopped pretending that I hadn't seen George's pants fall off when he was bowing and allowed my own emotions of embarrassed laughter to rock and roll. I began to laugh. Since I was carrying the food with both hands, ceremonially, to the front of the room, I couldn't stop to wipe my eyes or nose—liquid from these orifices was streaming down my face. The thought of my dripping face only made me laugh more. Now everyone to whom I served food began to laugh—whether or not they had seen George's pants fall off.

Laughter and tears are especially contagious when we have been softened by meditation. We experience our emotions more urgently after days spent in silent self-reflection. Emotions are exaggerated, and there is intimacy with others in the silent closeness. People told me later that they had not seen George's pants fall, but my laughing had set them off. Still we served the food, and those seated for the meal ate between giggles. I finished serving and removed the food bowls from the room.

When the meal ceremony concluded, I took the pots and serving bowls back to the kitchen. On my way, I found George sitting quietly on a bench in the garden. I had begun to wonder how he had survived his public humiliation, and I felt more than a little guilty for having laughed so intensely at his embarrassing revelation. Now a strong emotion of guilt was arising. I asked him if he was okay. He assured me that he was. To my eyes, he appeared to be beaming with calm and joy. He had lost his ego while naked in the zendo.

Sensing his stability, I asked him what happened. How had his pants fallen off? He said that they were held in place by a drawstring. When he felt the drawstring loosen, he took a big inward breath to puff out his belly and snug the pants. The inhalation had worked well for the first two bows, but the exaggerated inbreath had further stretched out the drawstring, and the pants had become even looser through his forced inhalation. What goes up must come down, and when he exhaled for the third bow, his waist circumference diminished. That's when the pants gave way. Deep breathing in the zendo is not always safe.

George twinkled when he told me that after he had pulled up his pants, he wanted to walk up to the front of the zendo. Then in his imagination, he would have stood before Sojun Roshi and announced, "Master, I have been enlightened." Looking at George's softly smiling face I had to agree with the validity of his intention. He had passed through the gate of public humiliation, and he had faced the loss of his ego's clothing. By announcing his awakening, he would have conveyed the wisdom of that moment to the entire community. He had gone beyond pants, no pants, and adult pride in wearing them properly. He was upright and fully present for the humiliating revelation. George was beaming peace and tranquility. Perhaps his experience could shed some light on the traditional Zen stories of enlightenment that occurred after a student's nose, arm, or pronouncement had been tweaked by the teacher. Pride in our own competence can be our largest obstacle to fully experiencing reality.

Indeed, something more had happened for George and for me, something more than the experience of a public humiliation. He had found his ease after his embarrassment. What was the meaning of this embarrassment? None of us wants to be that person who moons the zendo when bowing. Why do we fear our mistakes? What does public exposure mean to us? Does it make us less lovable? Does our self-image collapse? Will we lose our friends' respect? It seems to me that public humiliation might be as good as zazen for lessening the toxic effects of the ego. And considering how long it takes to lessen the ego's grip, humiliation may be one of the fastest and most effective Zen sangha practices.

George bestowed a teaching gift to me and to anyone willing to receive it. After George's pants fell off, I believed I could never achieve George's level of public embarrassment. But like George, I benefited by knowing that this level of disclosure was not only survivable but could also result in equanimity. George was the bodhisattva of humiliation; he had done what I was afraid to do. After George's pants fell off, I wondered how much of my energy went into protecting my self-image, and how much this self-protective energy blocked me from letting go of self-clinging. Through George's teaching example I achieved a new-found freedom from self-consciousness. I was more at ease in the zendo and elsewhere. I was confident that no matter how I failed, it would be difficult for me to top George. And if I actually could, I might become enlightened by my own act of public humiliation. Perhaps I had benefited deeply from my own embarrassing faint in the Tofukuji zendo.

Suzuki Roshi taught in *Zen Mind, Beginner's Mind*,

When we reflect on what we are doing in our everyday life, we are always ashamed of ourself . . . [quoting a student] "but the year has already begun and already I have failed."

Suzuki Roshi continued,

Dogen Zenji said *shoshaku jushaku. Shaku* generally means "mistake" or "wrong." *Shoshaku jushaku* means to succeed wrong with wrong, or one continuous mistake . . . A Zen master's life can be said to be *shoshaku jushaku.* This means so many years of one single-minded effort.

We spend hours practicing meditation, making great effort to reveal the truth about the present moment. Clearly the effort we make is not to "look good" or to be right or to avoid mistakes. For Zen students who focused on being correct, Suzuki Roshi had a term: "Looks like good." The single-minded effort is not to look good or be free from mistakes but rather to practice honestly and sincerely without trying to become good at it. Our practice of making mistakes, understanding our life is one mistake after another, is a single-minded effort. We don't stop practice when we make a mistake, we don't stop to think it should be otherwise. We keep practicing and let go of each mistake—apologizing when necessary. We can watch our mind try to reject, excuse, or erase a mistake, but we need to learn to let go of mistakes.

Because of George's emotional humiliation and his subsequent composure, I developed my own explicit Zen teaching about mistakes. At retreats I taught my students, "Make your mistakes often and publicly." I encouraged my students to do the most formal practice we could command as a sangha. But rituals were done with a different view. We did not perform ceremony to enact the form so that the ritual was performed exactly according to tradition. Instead, we aimed to complete the ritual perfectly while paying as much attention to the quality of our attention: the wavering attention leading to mistakes, our awareness of the mistakes, and our own reactions to the flub-ups. Whose fault was it that the food was cold? What about when the meal was served in the wrong order? When the chant leader has forgotten the chant? What then?

I taught my students that we didn't practice in order to do the rituals perfectly. We practiced with exquisite attention to the form so we could watch our mind noticing our mistakes and clinging to them in our favorite emotion. We want to become perfect by doing the ceremony perfectly. If we fail to enact the ritual correctly in front of the sangha, how do we meet this exposure, this embarrassment? Rituals became opportunities for me and our sangha to make mistakes in front of the community. We could honestly practice Dogen's *shoshaku jushaku* coming to life in our zendo. I could watch my mind wandering, making excuses and protecting my fragile ego.

Emotions energized the experience and made working through them more compelling. This is a most valuable teaching for a Zen community.

We can survey our self-criticism and self-reproach by watching our mind at any time of day. The practice of mistakes is useful all day long, in the zendo or out. But our self-consciousness and observing mind can be amplified by the hours of meditation with a witnessing audience. In any group spiritual practice, we combine increased attention with increased sensitivity. Performing in front of a group can be an emotionally vulnerable time. If you have opened a more spacious awareness, previously hidden emotional reactions and ego defense mechanisms become palpable. Emotions circulate in the body. Where do you feel embarrassment—in the body or the mind? Both places are stirred up. Noting that stirring, that circulating, can help us find settledness even within difficult emotions.

We can learn about the ways our mind grasps for "looking like good." Pride and egotism are vividly revealed through emotions. Spiritual practice within a peer group will help to heighten emotions. When we experience these strong emotions, we can circulate them in a larger space. The space we have amplified and that we share with our fellow practitioners can help us release and heal even strong habitual emotions.

16

TIGHT-ASS ZEN AND
WILD-ASS ZEN

I considered myself spiritually eclectic until I found myself at Tassajara for a hundred-day practice period. Welcome to the world of 24-7, all-day and everyday monastic Zen. One miserable morning at 3:00 a.m. early in the practice period, I realized I had married Zen. Even though I appreciated the wisdom in other traditions, it became clear to me that I had deeply entered the Zen way. Without my knowing, Zen had become the most reliable path for my spiritual development. At some point, unbeknownst to me, I had chosen Zen.

Sometimes, especially in the cold early morning, I cursed my choice. Every morning, awakened at that ungodly 3:00 a.m. hour, my first task was to take my still bed-warm body and place my tender buttocks on a frozen toilet seat. To compete with my lower body's shock and awe, I learned to scream. Loudly! The noisy creek, which ran under and chilled my cabin, drowned out the noise. The silence of the early morning was preserved, even as I screamed as loud as I could. Perhaps it was the daily cold ass and my wild screaming that introduced me to the notion of tight-ass Zen and wild-ass Zen.

After practicing for ten years at the Berkeley Zen Center, I was familiar with Zen's forms and rituals. I had cooked meals, served meals, cleaned the zendo, arranged the altar, rung the bells, led the chants, been head student for a practice period, and even served as president at that center. I had also practiced for a month in Japan at Rinso-in and had visited Eiheiji temple for a morning service. But in my mind, Tassajara's level of attention to detail bordered on an obsessive-compulsive disorder. By the end of the practice period, I understood why. I saw the opposition and balance of the two ways: tight-ass Zen maintained the daily schedule and practice. Wild-ass Zen made the practice rock and roll, straining and sometimes breaking Zen's reassuring tight container with humor and humanity.

It was at Tassajara that I learned my own inclination. It happened one morning when I was the designated chant leader. I was a newcomer, and all one hundred students present knew I had not yet memorized all the chants and their accompanying dedications. As fate would have it, my first morning as chant leader was accompanied by a generator outage. The zendo went dark. I could feel the tension rising. How would we complete the morning service? How could I lead the chants if I had no light to read the chant book? What would happen to our carefully choreographed day?

My natural impulse was to improvise. I moved from my position in the zendo as designated chant leader to a position by the altar, my chant leader's book in hand. There was a candle on the altar, and I hoped to read the chants by its light. I thought nothing of my improvisation. If you want to read, you find a light—simple, obvious, and effective. Later in the day during my afternoon hike, I kept meeting up with people who urgently asked me, "How did you know it was okay to stand by the altar?" I was puzzled until I realized that practice for some was always and only "by the book," with some vague danger lurking in any departure from the rules. Clearly there was no such danger in my way of practice.

But nothing would clarify the relationship of tight-ass Zen and wild-ass Zen at Tassajara like April Fools' Day. For me, pranking was a necessary requirement of any self-respecting Zen student. Show us your spirit! This was a way for all that practice awareness to circulate into community hilarity. As it turned out, during my practice period, April Fools' Day and the last day of the seven-day sesshin coincided.

On that April Fools' Day, the abbess, Zenkei Blanche Hartman, and all the Tassajara staff were serving food in the zendo. I organized a scheme ahead of time with my friends that would begin with me dropping my chopstick, followed by another twenty people who had agreed to drop one of their chopsticks on that signal. According to zendo protocol, the head meal server would need to pick up each chopstick individually, take it to the altar for ritual purification, and then ceremonially return it to its owner. This ritual worked fine when one chopstick per meal was dropped, but what chaotic hell realm would unfold with twenty of us dropping chopsticks simultaneously?

I expected to see tight-ass Zen driven mad. But the head server—and chopstick picker-upper—saw the big picture. After several chopsticks fell in quick succession, he simply ignored us and skipped the ritual of picking them up. The chaos I had schemed to create never materialized. Instead, we pranksters had to limp through our meal without the use of chopsticks. Since the head meal server was a true exemplar of precise tight-ass Zen, I was delighted to see he was not bound by the ritual. Within his respect for rules was common sense about the consequences of following them too tightly. His response showed his ability to obey or disobey the rules as the occasion necessitated. The beauty of wild-ass Zen and tight-ass Zen meeting in the monastery was a lively expression of Zen freedom. The pranksters were pranked.

Wild-ass Zen was expressed best by the outstanding Zen priest Ikkyu Sojun (1394–1481). After decades of monastic training, he found his own way through visiting brothels and wine shops and writing sensuous love poetry. After trying a stint as abbot of Daitokuji monastery in Kyoto, he resigned his position to escape the restrictions of monastic life and follow his appetites for women and raw shellfish. Later, after a temple-destroying fire, he was called back to rebuild Daitokuji, despite his unorthodox behavior. Ikkyu was honest about his behavior and expressed profound Zen understanding. For me, Ikkyu expresses wild-ass Zen and tight-ass Zen beautifully in the following poem from *Ikkyu and the Crazy Cloud Anthology: A Zen Poet of Medieval Japan*:

Every Day Priests Minutely Examine the Law

Every day, priests minutely examine the Law
And endlessly chant complicated sutras.
Before doing that, though, they should learn
How to read the love letters sent by the wind
and rain, the snow and moon.

Ikkyu describes the potential benefits to monastic practice through sensuous engagement with the natural world. He truly integrated his wild and sensuous nature with Zen wisdom. This is another example of circulating Zen awareness into poetry and love.

Chopstick Dharma combat was almost the highlight of a spirited April Fools' Day at Tassajara. But thanks to the efforts of one of my fellow wild-ass Zen partners, Junsei Jana Drakka, we surpassed the zendo play. Junsei decided to test my composure with a Zen ordeal of her own. In the monastery, one plans bathroom pee breaks with great care. After lunch was a great time to use my cabin's toilet. By afternoon, it had warmed up to an almost tolerable temperature—for an inhabitant of the Arctic Circle.

As a resident of a neighboring cabin, Junsei knew my habits. Imagine my surprise when I returned after April Fools' Day lunch to find my cabin door thoroughly locked up by duct tape. I knew immediately who had done it and laughed so hard that I wet myself before I could get the tape off the door. Junsei was seriously chastised by her supervisors (I didn't tell) for her mischievous use of duct tape. But like Ikkyu, her playfulness was integrated into her Zen teaching in her life beyond monastic training. Because she had practiced monastically, she brought authenticity to her teaching. Yet she retained enough adaptability to offer an appealing Zen teaching to a population of street people.

After Tassajara, Junsei continued her training with Zenkei Blanche Hartman. She spent many years offering ministry to low-income and homeless people. Through her street ministry, known on the streets of San Francisco as "The Zendo Without Walls," she offered meditation groups and counseling. She also did advocacy work on the board of Religious Witness with Homeless People. Junsei united diverse interfaith leaders with homeless people in the spirit of genuine compassion and the struggle for justice. Like other Zen masters before her, Junsei had a flexible mind and playful spirit, always knowing when to hold 'em and when to fold 'em when it came to the monastic rules and helping those in need.

When following a religion's rules, how do we create space to see not only the rules but also their meaning? The rituals and schedules we follow are important to help align us with the source of our spiritual training. But if following the rules becomes an end in itself, we may be alleviating anxiety by sticking to a routine that we think keeps us safe. We need to see what happens to our mind when the routine falls apart.

What then? We need to see the whole picture in the space of awareness, or we become imprisoned by spiritual practice rather than freed by it.

We may use practice routine to dull our mind and to ignore our anxiety. This is one way we may slip into spiritual bypassing instead of spiritual awakening. How do you use your spiritual community's rules? Rules are best used to build cohesion in the community and to encourage you to notice your reaction to the rules. Don't just follow the rules; create some space in your mind to watch your reactivity to rules. Watch your mind fighting the rules or loving the expert way you have mastered them. Circulate your awareness with your anxiety and/or pride.

17

THE SKY STARTS HERE

In the early days of Zen hippies, we thought we would become enlightened and live in some magical place. Now at practicing Zen centers, we believe we have become more practical in our aspirations. Now we understand that perhaps we will become enlightened, but at least we can have clean bathrooms and nutritious food. Maybe they are both the same wish. Something has changed over the years; Zen communities have encouraged practitioners to put full effort into their actual lives, jobs, and relationships. Zen has become more practical and interested in this moment's awareness circulated into everyday life. We may train at temples, observing traditional Zen rituals, but my Zen teachers have encouraged me to express spiritual practice by taking care of my actual life—my surroundings, my relationships, and my work.

Occasionally, even now at our more pragmatic Zen centers, people show up radiating the views of '60s hippies. At Zen retreats, we sometimes see people still believing there is an eternally blissful state in which they can safely reside. They often arrive looking like flower children and speaking in hushed tones that sound slightly drug induced. I usually avoid contact with these people—not wanting to be the one to burst the bubble. Soon enough, on their own, they will find out the difficult work required to follow a spiritual path. I'll wait until they land on the earth.

At one summer retreat, a lovely young woman fitting the above flower-child description came for a five-day meditation session. She was dressed as a '60s hippie and blessed us all with a beaming smile that seemed glued to her face. At the end of the retreat, each student asked the teacher a question in front of the community. The teacher answered in front of the community. This ceremony, expressing our communal experience, allows for further circulation of awareness in several ways.

First, each person reflects on how to create a statement. How do we find words that match the experience of spiritual awareness beyond words? Trying to do this without showing off or being a time hog is its own task of circulating awareness. Then there is the task of public speaking. How much self-consciousness do we feel sharing with fifty people? We become aware of that obstacle and we grapple with it when it is our turn to speak. Also, there is a shared experience with our fellow community members. Can we honestly express our questions, doubts, or shortcomings while taking care to not discourage others? All of these tasks help to circulate and integrate awareness into the emotional, social, and creative realms.

Many of the community's questions express the hardship of sitting meditation for five days and the struggle with unresolved questions or doubts. Some questions refer to the teacher's statements during Zen lectures. Students may ask follow-up questions if not satisfied with the teacher's initial answer. Sometimes the questions are intimate, sometimes superficial. All students show themselves, and the teacher tries to meet each student authentically. The teacher's depth is also revealed in the exchange.

I gathered more evidence for my snarky judgment when the young woman I had labeled "Bliss Mama" asked the teacher in a breathless and flighty tone, "Sojun Roshi, where do you live?" The question suggested that he resided in some other, more mystical dimension. I was surprised when my teacher answered her, "I live in the sky." He had met her expectation—that he lived on an elevated plane. Hearing his answer, she bowed to indicate she was satisfied, and that was the end of their exchange.

What puzzled me most was that my teacher had reinforced her magical view. I knew where he lived in Berkeley; he could have given his address or the Zen center address to root the question in reality. He met her fantasy instead; that baffled me. I carried my own belief about how a teacher should "help" a student. In my unrefined opinion, he should have straightened her out rather than encouraged her view that he was beyond the earth's gravitational pull. I couldn't see that he was meeting her where she was—"in the sky." I couldn't see the realm of possibility he had opened. If they connected in the sky, what could happen in this very big mind space?

Bliss Mama came back the following year to meditate for five days. When the time came for questions to the teacher, she referred back to the previous year's answer. She asked, "Last year when I asked you where you lived, you said you lived in the sky. What do you mean when you say 'I live in the sky'?" Without any hesitation, my teacher answered, "The sky starts here," as he pointed to the floor under his feet. I had not only underestimated the power of her inquiring mind but also misjudged my teacher's wisdom in meeting her where she was.

I found her question and his answer very satisfying. He didn't tell her that he was not magical, but he did let her know that he shared this human realm, the ground under our feet, with her. The answer also expanded the view of the sky. The sky is right here; it is not "up there somewhere."

The question also met the three requirements for answering a Zen question (*sanku*):

1. The cover (the answer) fits the box (the question)—the place where I live is right here.
2. The boat (the answer) rocks with the waves (the question)—the sky begins on the ground.
3. The answer cuts through the streams of delusion (of the questioner)—I am not special, and I do not live in a mystical land. I live here on the earth.

I was struck by the immensity of Sojun Roshi's answer. From the beginning, he understood Bliss Mama's thinking behind her original question—"Where do you live?" He met her in her own mystical realm—"I live in the sky." He had no need to correct her view, to insist that she land on our ordinary planet Earth. He gave her an enormous space in which to consider her question and his answer. His answer was all the more spacious because he knew that she did not live locally; she had come from out of town. He didn't know whether she would ever return to pursue her question. He didn't need to correct her Bliss Mama view of the world; he left that task to her. Did she wonder, "Does he really live in the sky? Can people live in the sky? Are there homes in the sky that I can't yet see? Is he kidding me about living in the sky?"

Clearly his first answer was a mystery to her, but she wanted to know its meaning. She was brave—she ventured to face him on the earth and in the sky. She found that my teacher did inhabit the sky, just as we all learned from that exchange that we all do. She was also living in the sky, she just did not know that. I did not know that I was living in the sky either. The meaning of sky, where we live, and our place on the earth were all placed in the great space of awareness.

The sky is a home where we can live and solve our deepest questions. He had made this sky available to her and to all of us listening. In this exchange, my awareness became awe. I saw my judgmental mind and I came to further understand my awareness of my life in the sky. We can look under our feet for the spacious sky when facing obstacles. The sky starts here, and there is room for everything.

18

SCHMUTZ ON THE WINDSHIELD

Zen centers are meant to be places where we find peace and practice compassion. But this is not always so. Personal relationships can be intensified, family conflicts relived, and old traumas reawakened within the community. This is an excellent opportunity to circulate awareness among old family wounds and the stubborn emotional reactivity left by early trauma. Within a spiritual practice community, amplified awareness can result in heightened sensitivity to relationship dynamics within the community.

I had been practicing at the Berkeley Zen Center for several years when a young woman joined the center. Most of the center's residents were long-term practitioners; she was new to Zen practice and had progressed to a residential commitment in a short time. She seemed to be a natural fit to meditation practice; she swam in its waters like a duck. But she also had a unique flair for conflict, and since she was new to practice, her ability to see herself reflected in the difficulty had not yet developed. For her, all feelings were caused by people and circumstances that were outside of her. Does that view sound familiar? She had many strong aversions to other women. I was soon singled out as a problem to her.

Before practice we blame everyone for our unhappiness. As we learn to watch our own mind, we can see more clearly, by our own reactivity, how much is on our side of the relationship and how much is being thrown our way by another. This discernment I call "schmutz on the windshield." How much schmutz is on the inside—our own view—and how much schmutz is on the outside of the windshield—thrown there by someone else? Either way, we need to discern and clear our view to move through the emotions that arise related to this schmutz. Discerning where the schmutz is—on which side of the windshield—is a way that circulated awareness can help with emotional wounds.

The divide between residents and nonresidents occasionally showed itself in financial policy at Zen centers. (Think, rent paid by residents but rent increases voted on by nonresidents.) However, conflict did not usually appear in personal squabbles. This generalization was not the case for her and the other women who irritated her. What concerned me most was when this young woman decided that she just couldn't stand being near me at Zen center meetings. I was told by Zen center officers to not sit next to her. The center's leadership obliged her dislike as if it were rational and meant to be indulged. Apparently, she hinted, her unresolved sister issues were triggered by other women "like her sister" practicing alongside her.

This dynamic is not so uncommon in some Zen centers. This can occur where women compete for the male teacher's attention and affection. Not surprisingly, the teacher may become an idealized daddy figure. Sometimes the teacher even encourages women to compete for their attention and affection. But I digress to an analysis; I really want to talk about what it is like to be hated. It was very difficult for me to be treated like a repulsive object that was not allowed to get too close to a person. It was painful to me when she would not make eye contact but instead looked away in disgust when I was in sight. I, like most people, am nourished by positive social cues. I feel hurt when another person sends nonverbal signals that I am not wanted. Ouch! Ouch!

At first I hoped to avoid the young woman's hate by expecting the Zen center leadership to teach her where hate came from and how to work with it. Instead they rationalized her insistence that I not sit next to her at meetings because it upset her. I was puzzled; after all, weren't we there practicing to come into harmony with what we feared and disliked? But the Zen center leadership offered their institutional support for her demands. I was told to neither sit next to her nor address her personally when we attended official Zen center meetings. Looking back, I suspect the Zen teacher's indirect intervention at the time was to introduce the chanting of the Metta Sutta within morning service. This particular chant reminded all of us of our responsibility—to pour compassion, love, and protection upon every being we encountered. I tried to do my part.

Since the Zen center was not going to help me avoid the "hate rays," I worked at finding ways to detoxify the hate. Could I use my own kindness? Perhaps I could convince my tormentor that I was, in fact, lovable. Do we doubt that we are lovable or worthy of love when someone hates us? Maybe I was trying to convince myself that I was actually lovable. She rejected all of my attempts at small acts of kindness, attention, and generosity. I was left wondering what I had done to deserve this treatment. Even worse, I was left wondering if I was just plain despicable. I was reminded of the poem "Vectors" by James Richardson, which describes hatred as a "night bombardment" that illuminates never-seen "places of myself." Being disliked can be a motivator to look deeply at your own part. What dark places could she see that I could not? I kept looking.

Reviewing one's own selfishness is a worthy task for a Zen practitioner, but keeping an open mind is really the essence of Zen. Looking in dark corners—corners you have painted black yourself—may not yield the most realistic answers. Looking and continuing to look without tainting perception is most useful. Finally, after much agonizing, the habit of looking straight ahead, without desire or fear, won the day and a valuable lesson was revealed. As taught by Master Hongzhi in *Cultivating the Empty Field*:

> Empty and desireless, cold and thin, simple and genuine, this is how to strike down and fold up the remaining habits of many lives. When the stains from old habits are exhausted, the original light appears, blazing through your skull, not admitting any other matters.

Just being nakedly disliked, not wanting to be liked, we can circulate awareness to move beyond these habitual emotional reactions. We can stop demanding that other people like us. We can stop insisting in our belief that we are lovable—or at least okay. Leaving the mind free of demands, empty and desireless, we may see what we had blocked previously. We can also see where the schmutz is clouding the windshield.

One early morning before 5:00 a.m. zazen, I must have been at least desireless, cold, and genuine. As I entered the gate to the Zen center, I saw the young woman who hated me on the zendo porch. There was a light illuminating her face in the darkness. She had her own light too; her face flushed with pleasure as she greeted another newly arrived meditator. She welcomed him with a smile to enter the zendo. My mind was empty, but still I took in the sweetness of the moment. A smile of sincere pleasure between two people with open hearts—simply beautiful.

In the next moment, the gate I had opened squeaked and her attention pivoted toward me. Her eyes fixated on my face. I believe I had a look of peace and serenity after witnessing her previous loving encounter. Maybe I looked more vulnerable than usual or maybe she imagined me needing her affection. As her eyes locked onto me in the early morning half-light, her face turned from a smile to a snarl. The direct experience was clear and stark; I could not deny its meaning. In that moment I was freed by my direct perception of reality. She hated me. It wasn't that we disagreed or were not on the same page. It wasn't that I had done something in particular. It was unmistakable; she hated me. It was as plain as the nose on my face! There was a light blazing through my skull with no other thoughts.

In that moment I dropped my belief in my own responsibility for her hate. I was emotionally unhooked from trying to fix it. Her hate was just her hate. Some people hate other races or nationalities. But she hated me! There was no need for me to understand why or how I might change her hate—it belonged to her. I let it go completely. I think, especially for women, we may struggle with a need to please. What is that need? How do we make our need to be liked someone else's problem? How do we keep asking others to provide us with the affection we need? Not coincidentally, when I let go of my objection to her hating me, within a week she let go of hating me. But, sadly, there was a long line of other female Zen practitioners who were to sequentially receive her same treatment.

This experience was neither the last time I have wondered why others don't like or welcome me, nor did it cure me of the initially intense pain of being hated. I remember being invited by a visiting Japanese roshi to a large Bay Area Zen center on a day he helped to plan a ceremony. As I walked in the door, a female leader said disdainfully and loudly enough for me to hear, "Who invited Grace? Why is she here?" While I felt the full force of her dislike and disapproval, my previous realization arose and continued to support my clarity. I exhaled, walked away, and remained free of the urge to explain or change her feelings. In fact, I had a realization about the occasional unfriendliness of Zen centers. The residents don't receive enough love from each other; how could I expect them to love me?

Practicing meditation and living in a Zen community do not necessarily cure us of our hindrances—greed, hate, and delusion. Some of us will self-reflect and receive training in projection and group dynamics. Others will continue to replicate the family of origin's cycles of like and dislike. Mistakes of sexual attraction and of hatred may continue unaddressed in the community. Watching the mind at work, our strong social and emotional needs may encourage growing awareness to address our reactions to schmutz both inside and outside of the windshield.

Besides learning to meditate, bow, and chant, how do we learn to understand our craving for personal love and our patterns of hate? How do we come to recognize and tame wild emotions? Integrating the realm of feeling emotions with the practice of letting go of emotions is a complex task. For the most part, this work does not occur magically in zazen—you have to be there for the pain and the release of the pain. Instead of thinking about the pain, reacting with hurt, shame, or anger, we need to step back into a more spacious relationship with our emotions. There is the world of difference in saying "anger is arising" instead of "I am angry." When you say "anger is arising," you have space around the anger. It is not just you, up close and identified with the anger. There is space for movement. Entering the space you have cultivated, you may find the necessary release.

I am hoping that Zen centers in the West will recognize the need to acknowledge the roots and reenactments of strong personal feelings within community. Meditation and chanting will not necessarily address personal traumas and reactivity to other people. How can we integrate psychological understanding, referrals to therapy, and clearer behavioral guidelines into Zen center curriculum? Adding our contemporary perspectives on human behavior does not take away from traditional training in meditation. Circulating spiritual practice and awareness into personal longing provides clarity to difficult emotional reactivity.

There is a story about how a Japanese Zen temple community greeted a young priest who arrived at a time when he was the only new student. Knowing the importance of peer friendship and how much peers can support each other through the initial hardships of practice, temple leadership pondered his difficult situation of entering temple life alone. They decided to sneak candy under his meditation cushion from time to time to let him know that he was seen and (secretly) loved. The new monk would find treats under his cushion, but there would be no note to indicate who had left the candy for him. There was an atmosphere of care surrounding him in the midst of his rigorous training. Appreciating the necessity of friendship can become part of traditional training. First we need to become aware of the importance of emotional and social bonds. I think we would do well to actively dispense more candy, more caring at Western Zen centers. Until we do, the absence of demonstrable affection within Zen communities may reinforce harmful mental habits. Our job is to bring awareness to strong emotions.

19

DOES A BUDDHA HAVE
DOG NATURE?

Where East and West Meet

Earlier I mentioned the koan "Does a dog have Buddha-nature?"
The answer is Mu—no, no thing, or no thingness. When my
eleven-year-old son, Kern, met Hoitsu Suzuki Roshi at the
Berkeley Zen Center, the question arose in mirror image: "Does
a Buddha have dog nature?" This question asks whether a Zen
master can express the unbounded joy and unfailing friendliness of a happy puppy.

Hoitsu Suzuki Roshi was the son of Shunryu Suzuki Roshi.
He continued his father's work supporting American Zen practice. He came to the Berkeley Zen Center to encourage us and
to support Sojun Roshi and the community. Kern had watched
Hoitsu Suzuki Roshi interacting with members of the BZC
community and immediately sensed something distinctive
about his overflowing cheerfulness.

On our way home in the car, Kern began to giggle. Kern
often had a way of intuiting emotions, feeling them as if he
were being tickled. Kern announced, "He's like a baby," sensing
Hoitsu Suzuki Roshi's direct access to expressing joy. Then
Kern was quiet for a few moments, as he continued to roll

this idea over in his mind. "No," he said. "Babies cry, so he is not like a baby."

What Kern sensed at the Zen center and struggled to express in words was something I had experienced when I stayed at Hoitsu Suzuki Roshi's home temple in Japan. I was there training with a group of eleven other Zen women from California. Hoitsu Suzuki Roshi enjoyed teaching us ceremony, enjoyed his sake and sushi, enjoyed his parishioners, and broke into fits of giggling when he explained to our visiting Zen practice group that the puddle we had found on the tatami in the Buddha Hall was "animal pee-pee." He also shook with laughter when he told us how scary it was to take American women shopping for used kimonos. While Zen Buddhist women may shun shopping in theory, finding beautiful and shockingly inexpensive Japanese used clothes seemed to remove all constraints. Hoitsu Suzuki Roshi laughed out loud as he described the kimonos flying through the air as twelve of us rooted for treasures in the piles of used clothing.

Hoitsu Suzuki Roshi's temperament was more than a simple matter of biology. We had learned to meditate and chant in American Zen temples, but Hoitsu Suzuki Roshi's joy was a different kind of training that we Americans had missed and sorely needed. We came to understand our deficit after our first week of practicing with him. Unaccustomed to foreign visitors, the townspeople of Yaizu, where the temple was located, were curious about us. They seemed to regard us as a cross between movie stars and dragons, both glamorous and frightening in our strangeness.

One morning Hoitsu Suzuki Roshi gathered all twelve women together for instruction. He explained by starting slowly: "Because you are practicing here at Rinso-in, you are now nuns of this temple. This is how the people in Yaizu see you when you go into the village. They see you as nuns of

Rinso-in." Fair enough; we had seen ourselves as practitioners when in the temple, and as Zen tourists when in town. He continued: "When you pass people in Yaizu, you should say *ohaiyo gozaimasu* (good morning) or *konichiwa* (good day), and you should smile at them. Smile? Many of us from Zen centers in Berkeley thought our facial expression and demeanor should express seriousness and suffering.

Hoitsu Roshi taught us that if Zen practice doesn't create and share peace and joy, what good is it? If your Zen practice is not friendly and encouraging of the people you meet, what good is it? Here was a teaching that shined the light of awareness on human emotions and the need to lift others. His comments awakened us to a different view of practice. Zen was not just for us to contemplate our own existence—however deep and dark the questioning might be. In fact, the practice of smiling is one of the simplest enactments of Zen's bodhisattva vow "to save all beings."

Practice meant something different in a society that had been supporting Zen nuns and priests for almost a thousand years. Japanese people were not supporting an endless self-referent or self-absorbed inquiry. They were supporting the development of unselfish, kindhearted, and friendly clergy. How quickly we learned the essence of their practice: kindness. Practice could transform humans into suffering-converting equipment. We could create a suffering-transforming device: into the awakened body goes the suffering; out comes the love. We were to train ourselves to meet all people with friendliness and encouragement.

In the car driving home from Kern's first meeting with Hoitsu Roshi, after a few moments of further silent reflection, Kern announced, "I know, I know! He is like my dog, Albert." Albert was our black Lab puppy whose abundant joy leaped out everywhere he went. When we took Albert for obedience training, we needed to use a stiff and barbed choke collar because, in the words of the dog trainer, "To this dog, every sensation feels like petting." I had regular calls from the staff at Lake Merritt whenever Albert escaped the yard to chase ducks in the cold lake. Albert knew how to enjoy his life to the fullest, and his joy was contagious.

So let us fully appreciate the dog nature of the Buddhas. However one may struggle with the famous koan—"Does a dog have Buddha-nature?"—it is abundantly clear that a true Buddha has dog nature: friendly, cheerful, bounding with joy. As we welcome Zen to the West, let us remember the importance of expressing dog nature in Buddhist practice. Tail wagging, smiling, loyal friendship, and greeting and meeting beings with joy and affection is a wonderful outcome of meditation training and a goal for all of us humans.

Part Four

Zen Goes Live at Home

A Little Zenderness

Each part of this book shows the process through which spiritual awareness is discovered, amplified, circulated, and finds its freedom in your life. This sky-mind, or awareness, is the self-reflective quality of the mind that can grow in brightness, focus, depth, and quality. Awareness is what observes your mind thinking, sometimes called the observing self or the essence of mind. I have described my own discovery of this essence from childhood bliss, trauma, and finding Zen with Suzuki Roshi. More importantly, wisdom is a light we can share. How does each person use their own life lessons to wake up and live fully? I have heard Charlotte Joko Beck conclude that if you don't use your practice in your life off the cushion, it is better not to sit down and meditate at all. I have also heard Dzogchen Ponlop Rinpoche advise that formal practice on the cushion is like reading a software instruction manual—you may read the manual, but you don't learn how to use the software until you try to do your work on your computer.

This part, "Zen Goes Live at Home," describes the fourth step in developing awareness. Outside of formal practice settings, without a training environment or a formal teacher, in the midst of emotional triggers, awareness practice of expanded mind can bubble up in your personal struggles and family life. While feeling strong emotions with family, the current task is to cultivate an ability to use awareness freely. After amplifying and circulating awareness, you have gained confidence in the reliability of realization at this stage. You can begin to trust your life to the awakened mind you have been cultivating. You can allow awareness to guide you instead of relying on ingrained habitual reactions. Awareness is free to inform and move within your family life.

20

THE HONORABLE BULLY
CAT ROSHI

In his commentary in *From the Zen Kitchen to Enlightenment*,
Uchiyama Roshi, a Japanese teacher in my Soto Zen tradition,
teaches that "everything you encounter is your life." He also
taught that "we throw our whole lives into whatever we encounter, and that is the attitude of living." This is not just a
teaching about accepting the good *and* the bad circumstances
as they appear in your life. If everything is your life, you
need to be in the very middle of your life to understand it.
Before you can have a view of what action to take, of how to
respond, how do you fully inhabit this moment? If you separate what you encounter into categories of what belongs or
doesn't belong in your life, your responses will be prejudicial
and inadequate.

When my sons were seven and ten years old, we got two
cats—Magnus and Tiger. Each boy claimed one cat as his pet.
The cats lived with us in Boston during graduate school, then
moved with us to Los Gatos in the South Bay area of California, and finally resettled with us in our East Bay home when
the boys were eleven and fourteen. Our homes changed and
the cats came along, a source of family stability while we were
on the move.

The cats spent time outdoors and came inside the back porch at night or when the weather was wet. My husband, Peter, was allergic to cats, so they weren't allowed to roam the house as the boys and I had intended. But they seemed content enough; they enjoyed the sun on the back deck and were let in to the back porch when they called out. But life with pets always delivers unexpected challenges.

One day we heard a noisy cat scuffle and lots of caterwauling on our back deck. There we found the largest calico tomcat I had ever seen. He appeared to rule the roost—gobbling up our pets' food and chasing them into hiding below our deck. Magnus and Tiger seemed terrified. I wasn't far behind as the cat hissed and sprayed at my approach. There was no longer peace in our cat realm. I shooed the calico tom away and retrieved Magnus and Tiger, hoping that encounter would be the end of it. But it wasn't the end of Bully Cat's reign of terror—not even close. Bully Cat made himself at home in our yard, complete with our cat food, bowls of water, and our sunny back deck.

The boys and I discussed our options. How would we drive the intruder, Bully Cat, from the yard? We desperately wanted to protect Magnus and Tiger and their territory. We yearned for a return to cat peace and harmony, and we wanted an end to this new and uninvited household conflict. We decided to target Bully Cat with unpleasant experiences. First we tried yelling and shooing with a broom, but Bully Cat only retreated a few steps. Then we tried chasing him away with water. He would slink off to a safe distance, then return to the porch. The next step was to target Bully Cat with a squirt gun loaded with cayenne pepper and water. He simply licked it off. Magnus and Tiger were in hiding, unable to eat or sun on the back porch. Bully Cat was there to stay.

So the boys and I had another conference to explore possible new tactics to shoo Bully Cat away. School and work schedules kept us away from home during the day, so we needed to leave cat food and water outside for Magnus and Tiger. Because we didn't want to hurt Bully Cat, our options for driving him off were limited. We watched him in the yard as he finished off our cats' food and strutted back and forth in the sun. Contemplating Bully Cat at his ease shocked my point of view. Bully Cat was relaxed and happy because he thought he was at home. He thought he was *our* cat. I had encountered my whole life, as in Uchiyama's teaching, and it included Bully Cat.

I shared my realization with my sons. "Oh my God, Bully Cat thinks he's *our* cat!" I said. The boys gasped, entering Bully Cat's point of view. "He thinks he belongs to us! He thinks this is *his* house and we are his family." Suddenly we saw our own awful behavior through Bully Cat's eyes. Why was he not loved and welcomed like Magnus and Tiger? Why did we try to scare him, to make his life miserable? The three of us now acknowledged how terrible our own behavior must have appeared to him. He was an abused and unloved cat.

Both of my boys had tears in their eyes as they realized that Bully Cat thought he belonged to us, just as our own cats belonged to us. Our cats had a loving family, but Bully Cat had a mean one. From the beginning, we had been seeing Bully Cat strictly from our self-referent perspective; we had not seen ourselves or our aggressive tactics through the cat's eyes. When we let go of our fixed view, we saw Bully Cat's mistreatment within our own family clearly. How could he possibly know he wasn't *our* cat?

In that instant, unbidden, Uchiyama Roshi's simple expressions and his meaning shocked me: "Everything you encounter is your life. We throw our whole lives into whatever we encounter, and that is the attitude of living." Bully Cat was also our life and our cat. He did not exist outside of an imaginary circle we had drawn around our family. We were meeting our life through him, and his experience of us was also our life.

From the first moment I met Bully Cat, I had decided he was not part of my life, even as he insisted that he was. I did not make space in my life for his actual existence. Until I could understand Bully Cat's persistent position in the middle of my life, I could not solve the problem. Pushing him away was not going to change his mind or his behavior. Bully Cat had been through tough times before, and he knew how to survive the mistreatment. He couldn't stay with us in our home, but our program for driving him away with water, shooing, and a broom would never work. Our simple decision that he didn't belong in our life wasn't working. We needed to see that his intrusion was part of our life.

Bully Cat was rather large and liked to hiss, and I feared he would scratch me if I tried to contain him. Once I understood Bully Cat's point of view, I had the space to consider an actual solution that would work for all of us. First I needed to get help from an animal rescue group to remove him from our yard. Then with some research we were able to send Bully Cat to a more appropriate environment. Bully Cat Roshi had taught us to look at the whole picture and to see how all of us interacted from our own personal view—cat or human. Perhaps this lesson of stepping into the other's view—the cat's-eye view—helped my sons become successful managers in their work lives. But that's another story.

21

Sand and Rice

Creating family life is like cooking an original meal made of yourself—all your personal ingredients combined with those of your child. Your personal strengths and weaknesses, genetic likeness, the way you were raised—all these ingredients are in the gumbo. The cooking pots are the loving relationship. In addition to the ingredients you started with, your influence and your child's personhood begin to complete the dish, and the whole cuisine is spiced with discipline, humor, and your principles. Sometimes the dish that emerges stuns the cook. Sometimes it is neither what you expected nor how you wished it to turn out. Other times, your child emerges, declares his or her own wisdom beyond your influence, and the dish you cook blows you away.

In Zen, the teacher as spiritual parent tests how the student's understanding is ripening. In some Zen stories, the teacher samples and seasons the student's understanding only to discover that the student has surpassed the teacher. Like every child, every Zen student ripens to become his or her own unique creation. One old teacher, Tozan, walking through the busy monastery kitchen to check his student Seppo the cook, asked a puzzling question. "When you are washing the rice, do you wash the sand and pick out the rice or do you wash the rice and pick out the sand?" The student answered, "I wash and throw away both the sand and the rice together." Tozan asked, "Then what on earth do the residents here have to eat?" In response, Seppo turned over the rice bucket, throwing away all the ingredients. To waste food in a Zen kitchen is more than a mistake; it is a serious violation. Tozan calmly observed, "The day will come when you will practice under another master."

Tozan was not emotional or punitive, but he was calmly observing that this student's behavior and understanding were a handful—maybe not amenable to Tozan's own style. This was a student who went beyond Tozan's verbal questioning, putting his whole heart into his answer. Seppo was unafraid of the consequences of turning over the bucket and throwing away the food; Seppo's understanding and temperament took him beyond words. Tozan, a mature teacher, understood the power of Seppo's answer, but he was not sure he was the right teacher to meet Seppo's force.

Like the old master checking his student in the kitchen, many conversations between parent and child explore just what is sand, what is rice, and how the child might distinguish which behaviors to keep and which to throw away. A parent may think they can easily identify what is of value, distinguishing between rice and sand, and offer clear instructions to the child on how to separate the two. But we often distinguish rice from sand through the clouded lens of our defenses developed in response to personal pain. We try, perhaps unconsciously, to be right, to protect our point of view. We may justify or rationalize according to our own values, but the child may have a different view. Sometimes it is our child who helps us see through our limitations in a dramatic act of kicking over our bucket of ideas.

In one such situation, it was my fourteen-year-old son, Max, who threw over the bucket. It was a painful conversation: his father and I had decided to separate. Of course, in such a conversation, adults may try to talk about the "very good reasons." Max knew the sand quite well—our arguments and unhappiness. He'd witnessed more than enough. The rice we offered was the planned separation, a newly constructed living arrangement, and a pledge to love and support him in the new configuration.

In one fell swoop, Max threw over the bucket, its contents, the conversation, and our rationalizations. After listening carefully and quietly to our decision, Max said calmly, "No matter what you say or do, I have lost my family. And I will never, ever, get my family back." His father and I hung our heads in silent shame. There was no arguing with his no-nonsense expression of loss, the failure of both parents. We were humbled. This was Max's loss, and his strength and wisdom came forward to bear his suffering. Allowing his wisdom and suffering to stand unanswered was our parently act of courage; no arguing, no defensiveness, our silence validated his experience. Thirty-five years later, I weep recalling his words and the pain he refused to hide.

In fact, when my husband and I reconciled after our separation, we got another comeuppance from Max. After a year's separation, Peter and I found out that our own unhappiness was just that, and our love and married life were worth more effort. When we sat down with fifteen-year-old Max to tell him we were getting back together, he had this to say: "When I worried about your fighting, you told me that you wouldn't divorce. I accepted that. When you told me that you were divorcing, I accepted that. Now you are telling me that you are getting back together. How will I ever trust you again?" In that moment, I heard the sand, rice, and bucket rolling across the floor.

In such a moment, when your child points out your failures and inadequacies, what will you do? In that moment, can you wait with the pain without defensive maneuvering? Where will you find the space, the open mind within which you can wait with your pain as you take in your child's experience? Finding the space to let go of your reactivity for the sake of your child's experience takes a practice of self-reflection. One must build a relationship to this space; one has to have confidence in this space as a place to heal. One needs a relationship to expanded awareness to begin to accept such a painful view.

There is always the possibility that the child's expressed view is extreme and even incorrect, but will your arguing about it help in the moment? In our particular situation, because Max's father and I eventually reconciled and did not divorce, maybe he did get his family back. Certainly he did not return to a family that he could trust as he had before. Max later created his own substantial family, with a wife and three children. But the truth of that earlier moment, the power of a dissident child's independence and realization, was a vivid expression of his autonomous strength. He had kicked over our bucket.

The act of throwing over the bucket means that one cannot rely on and be guided by another's ideas and concepts held within any situation. Sometimes the ideas can be refined, but sometimes the whole structure must be scrapped to find fresh growth. Max went on to a business career where he helped launch a successful software firm. He studied bridge and has won championships. He has been faithfully married for twenty-two years, and alongside his wife, he is raising his three children. He is guiding his eldest son through college selection. He is sharing his home with his aging parents. A total rejection of the sand and rice is sometimes the only appropriate response on the path to clarity, autonomy, and a deeper connection.

Seeing Max shape his stable home and work life, I have been inspired by the path he created beyond what he was given and beyond his own suffering. And perhaps now I better understand what Tozan meant when he told Seppo that he would one day study under a different master. Max, too, has matured under his own master.

22

You Exist,
Therefore I Am Embarrassed

Parenting is an act of studying oneself and one's child in relationship. Eihei Dogen taught that "to study the Buddha Way is to study the self. To study the self is to forget the self. To forget the self is to be actualized by myriad things." When we are looking carefully at our own characteristics and shortcomings in a relationship, how do we forget the self and make room for the reality of the other side of the relationship? By asking and looking at our own self through another's eyes, we may encounter other possibilities as our self. Maybe I am too this or too much that. Can we allow the whole self to be part of the bigger picture of the way the world is changing? Can we take our focus off the small self, which we have been polishing to be perfect? Several experiences with my younger son, Kern, helped bring these questions to life.

Anyone who has raised children knows how cute they are when they are small, and how challenging they are when they are teenagers. Somewhere in the process we become different to them. Once we were needed and lovable, but at some point we become unbearable. It doesn't happen all at once, but we gradually take our cues from dirty looks, slammed doors, and being shunned around their friends. Some children seem to form their independence by pushing us aside.

My younger son was remarkably articulate on this matter throughout his teenage years. His wisdom shone even while I was teaching him to drive (a true test of parental love). I helped to teach both of my sons to drive on my stick shift. But by the time I taught my second son, I was not willing to sacrifice my clutch—again. So it came to pass one day, as he tried to start the car from a dead stop parked on a hill, that my clutch was in danger. I made a pronouncement: "You have three tries to start this car, pull away from the curb, and move up the hill. If you can't get this car driving up the hill, I will take over and move the car up the hill to a level spot. Then you may resume the lesson back in the driver's seat."

After the third try, I changed places with him and moved the car off the hill. Of course, even if we had been on our own, this event would have been embarrassing enough to any teenage boy whose mom could accomplish feats of driving that he couldn't. But there was a witness in the car—my son's best friend. My son, not one to pitch an infantile fit, revealed the conflict of Mother besting him at driving with his wry sense of humor. Addressing his friend, as I drove up the hill, he proclaimed dryly, "I taught her everything she knows." His friend laughed, and we continued our lesson. For a young man, being bested by Mom must have a special place in the hell realm. I have often marveled at how, in that situation, my son fully understood and mastered his vulnerability so efficiently.

He did not waste words when describing my place in his world. He was actively learning how this mom-son thing worked. He paid attention when he was with friends and their families, and he recounted what he observed. He told me once that my problem was that I was both smart and mean when compared to other friends' mothers who were "kinda dumb and nice." He went on. "Take Don's mother, for example. When he asked her for money for the movies, she gave him a twenty," he explained. "Then Don said, 'Mom,' with disgust in his voice. And she said, 'Sorry,' and gave him another twenty." My son Kern said proudly or ironically, "You would never fall for that. You'd tell me to go get my allowance." He saw his friends in similar struggles, and he was doing comparative analysis. I took it as a compliment. After all, you may only get an indirect few—if any—from your teenager.

My son's grasp of his growing-up dilemma was speedy, penetrating, and articulate. In high school, he was becoming a man—strong and independent. And yet there I was—living proof of his dependence and his earlier vulnerability. The journey to manly independence, while being loved, often requires distancing Mom. When he was a teen, I repeatedly watched his discomfort when we were together near his friends. Nevertheless, in a private moment I tried to reconcile how difficult it was for him to have an actual mother. I stated my own appeal for personal guidance. "Please let me know if anything I do embarrasses you."

Once again, his answer—swift, to the heart of the matter, and uncompromising: "Mother, the fact that you exist embarrasses me." Even in that moment I found relief and humor in his words. His discomfort with me wasn't personal; it was generic. I didn't need to be on guard for my annoying voice tones or my inability to appreciate sports. In fact, it wasn't any of my oh-so-many actual flaws but rather the essential fact of our relationship. He was a man, born of a woman's body, and he was trying to establish his manhood. How could he become fully independent and remain connected to me?

When participating in the change from parenting a child to parenting an adult, we are wise to consider how we can let go of the fixed self, how we can find the space for change.

Using Eihei Dogen's teaching, how do we forget the self that is center stage? How do we see ourselves as one of the ingredients in the soup, as one taste in the soup? The essence of the soup is defined by how we blend with or bring out the flavors of others. Our life is a blend of relationships. Can we actually see how others regard us in relationship? First, we must relax that tight grip on self-image. What if we find a neutral space within that we can check our own self-image alongside the view held by another? This view is required when practicing awareness within the family.

Then, if we can return to a spacious mind, we can see how tightly we cling to the self for which we want to be acknowledged. Sometimes we can glimpse how this self looks to others. Those two views—how we see ourselves and how others see us—are most likely to be different. But the exercise of holding the two views of who we are side by side may help loosen the grip with which we cling to our own self-image. In that amazing moment, even with a view offered by our challenging teenagers, we may glimpse our freedom to let go of that firm belief in self-image. An opportunity to be free from habits and defenses.

Now when I tell people what my son said to me when he was fifteen, I get two reactions. First, horror that he could be so mean (well, perhaps he did come by it honestly). How could he talk to his mother that way? How could he dismiss the importance of the relationship? The second reaction is one of admiration. He found a way to speak of his angst without putting me down for the actual millions of ways I irritated him. He might have said, "Mom, there are just too many things you do to embarrass me, I am not going to even get started." That was also most likely true, but what he said to me was infinitely wiser and kinder. Yes, I was so embarrassing, it was hard to even get started. But looking deeply, all the way to the bottom, it was not me in particular. It was the fact that there was an "us." We existed in this relationship—not one, but not quite yet two independently.

Those who see the remark as mean may be reacting emotionally, imagining how they would have felt if their own child declared them to be embarrassing in every instance, 24-7. I understand how painful it can be to raise teenagers, and I have felt that agony. For those who can see the clarity in his remark, I appreciate your philosophical bent, your ability to free yourself—even momentarily—within the dilemma of parenting. There is a large container for us parents; it holds a lifetime of relating. We need to see the relationship existing in a large space. The relationship exists in the shared view of the self and who we are to one another. Rumi writes:

Out beyond ideas of wrongdoing and rightdoing,
there is a field. I'll meet you there.

In university, Kern majored and excelled in philosophy. But I am not sure if he ever surpassed his first dictum: "You exist, therefore I am embarrassed."

23

DIAL M-O-M FOR JUSTICE

Zen has helped me channel my passion for justice into acts that may be useful in addressing injustice. I lived in a tent in Canada for four years in protest of the Vietnam War, but I am now housebroken. I still attend protests, but I try hard to not get arrested since I know they won't serve me gluten-free food in jail. In my seventh decade, I also understand my many limitations, and I work to encourage others, who share my views, to protest injustice. How well my son Kern understood my tendency to yell "Unfair!" whenever I encountered injustice. How well he exploited my tendency to protest loudly and actively. Astute as he was, Kern made use of my knee-jerk response—"Unfair, unfair, unfair!"

Especially, I remember the time that Kern enlisted me to protest an unfair ticket he received for a moving violation—crossing the double yellow line—near the police station in our small community. "Mom, there is *no* double yellow line where I got this ticket!" he exclaimed. Because he was under eighteen, we both needed to appear in person at the juvenile court. We scheduled the hearing—a hearing that would decide whether he could continue to drive or not. In order to properly prepare for the hearing with the juvenile officer, I immediately drove us to the scene of the purported crime to take a picture. Kern knew well how to engage the justice seeker in his mom.

Just as Kern had described, there was no double yellow line on the road in that location. I took the photographs and felt prepared to help present his case. While the ticketing officer may also appear in court to validate their claims, the officer did not come that day. I showed the judge the photographs and the ticket was removed from Kern's record—that time. Kern went on to accrue other tickets, and we even attended traffic school together. Going around the traffic school classroom, when he was asked for what offense he was required to attend traffic school, he pointed to me, sitting next to him, and said, "Because that's my mom!" Some thanks for parenting and all the services provided.

But later I predictably yelled again "Unfair, unfair, unfair!" Twenty years after I protested Kern's ticket, I discovered the truth about the ticket he had received for crossing the double yellow line. He and another friend had decided to drag race in the short space of road near the police station. The police officer, in his infinite kindness, wrote two tickets—one for each of the two young men racing near the civic center—for crossing the double yellow line and not for reckless driving. This information came to me twenty years after the fact, after my efforts in juvenile court on Kern's behalf. Yes, there was no double yellow line. And yes, they had crossed a line. There was more information strategically withheld. Unfair, unfair, unfair!

This reminds me of a Zen story in case 75 in the *Blue Cliff Record*. A monk came from Joshu's assembly to meet Ukyu, who asked him if Joshu's teaching was different than what he had found with Ukyu. The monk answered that nothing was different. Ukyu told the monk to go back to Joshu, and he hit him with his stick.

The monk then said, "If your stick had eyes to see, you would not strike me like that." Ukyu said, "Today I have come across a monk." And gave him three more blows. The monk turned back and said, "To my regret, the stick is in your hand." Ukyu said, "If you need it, I will let you have it." The monk went up to Ukyu, seized his stick, and gave him three blows with it. Ukyu said, "Unfair blows! Unfair blows!" The monk said, "One may receive them." Ukyu said, "I hit this one too casually." The monk made bows. Ukyu said, "Osho [teacher]! Is that how you take leave?" The monk laughed aloud and went out. Ukyu said, "That's it! That's it!"

Whether responding to Zen students or helping one's children, don't be so automatic, so predictable; don't give a stereotyped response. In this situation, Ukyu used his tried-and-true usual response—hitting with the stick. Then he regretted that he had not been more original with this promising student who did not stay to learn from him. He missed this opportunity, and he expressed disappointment. When Ukyu watched this student leave, he knew he had missed the big picture—the potential offered by this student's challenge. He missed giving an original and truly deep response. How do we stay connected to the context and to our own tendencies? No matter how hard we try, I suspect we will be tricked; we will receive the unfair blows.

As a parent, I have meted out a similar standard "Go to your room" and "You're grounded" consequences for my two sons, from when they were five years old through their teenage years. Before they were age five, I delivered three hits to their well-covered rear ends with a wooden spoon. However, when all the wooden spoons disappeared from my kitchen, I got the message that they had outgrown my use of the stick.

They had taken the stick from me at an early age. Just as we teach our children, they teach us; sometimes the teachings are fair, and sometimes not. But like Ukyu, we need to know when we have met our match. Apparently the stick had been in my sons' hands much earlier than I realized.

Whether or not we face a change in or an inevitable challenge to authority, how do we take a stance without relying on an automatic or knee-jerk response? We remember that there is no substitute for being present with full awareness. We call up our awareness—developed through years of communicating with it—to stay present in each situation and not give in to our tendencies. We start to also become more aware of the automatic behaviors we have relied on for many years. It is difficult to slow down the ingrained habitual response when faced with a situation that matches our habit so well; it is tempting to fit the ready response to the situation. The brain loves the efficiency of using what we have done in the past—the habits have become part of our neurological circuitry. It feels almost magnetic, and it is important to feel that feeling when it arises in the body or in retrospect through asking, "What just happened?"

By reflecting on our own process, we can make use of a more spacious mind and know what it feels like when that ready response arises. What is your familiar feeling? You may become aware of a little glee or buzz in the body when the automatic response comes forward and kicks into place. Does it carry a triumphant tone: "I've got this"? Can you detect an inner smirk? Only you can know what the subtle undercurrent of feeling is in your own body-mind equipment. While it is hard to detect these rapidly emerging and fleeting feelings in an exciting moment, they are easier to recognize in quieter moments. That's why we practice and develop awareness in the quieter moments—we build the muscle of awareness for the times our impulses are strong.

Whether it is the legal system, a student, or our offspring, how do we adjust to the inevitable unfair blows? As a Zen teacher, mother, mother-in-law, grandparent, and protestor, I have learned about the unfair blows. They can sting, but the lesson we learn is how to respond effectively to the hurt. An automatic "I'll save the day" or an angry response probably won't help.

I have learned to first say "Ouch," sometimes only to myself. I try to not hit back—it may be momentarily satisfying but is not usually helpful to initiate change. I review what preceded the unfair blows. I try hard to see my part. Stopping to see what has occurred is helpful in holding back a habitual response in favor of generating an appropriate response. Being able to generate an appropriate response was described by the Chinese Zen teacher Yunmen as the ultimate teaching of the Buddha's entire lifetime.

Another guide to responding to the inevitable confrontation with our mistaken automatic response teaches the necessary humility and acceptance, as illustrated in case 13 of *The Gateless Barrier*. One day Tokusan came toward the refectory from the Meditation Hall, carrying his bowls. Seppo called out to him, "Where are you off to with your bowls, when the bell has not rung and the drum has not been struck?" Without a word, Tokusan went at once back to his room. The old teacher, when corrected by his student, took the correction gracefully. No excuses such as "I thought I heard the bell" or "So-and-so told me it was time." He just silently changed direction.

Whether tricked by your mind, tricked by your son, or tricked by a political process, please work to see the whole picture. Don't miss the chance to see yourself in context. Let yourself be present and connected; too many automatic responses leave us open to ineffective actions, more mistakes, and further trickery. But sometimes the learning will occur after the fact.

24

MY GRANDDAUGHTER

Zen Master Olivia Teaches
Zen Master Myogen about Death

Olivia is Max's youngest daughter, one of three grandchildren with whom we share a house in California. When she was just four years old, she helped me understand death. I was standing in my kitchen cooking, Olivia was drawing, and she suddenly spoke up. "Grandma, you are going to die," she said confidently. "Everyone dies," she added with a proud and knowing certainty. I was quite interested in where this conversation was going. Lucky for both Olivia and me, I was a Zen person who had contemplated my own impermanence. Otherwise, I might have been flustered into heart palpitations or, at the very least, bothered into a sharp gasp and a potential reprimand for Olivia's impertinence.

"You are right, Olivia," I responded. "What will we do about this?" She answered me with the same cool confidence with which she had pronounced the certainty of my death: "Even after you die, Grandma, we will still be together," Olivia reassured me. Curious about both her certainty and her understanding of our relationship after my demise, I asked Olivia, "Do you think we will talk to each other after I die?" She pondered my question briefly before she replied comfortingly, "No, Grandma, but we will think of each other." And that was that. Olivia went back to her drawing.

I was astonished by her brief sermon, and I thought about why I love Zen. I don't love Zen for the robes and the folderol; I love it for where the rubber meets the road—whether in my own kitchen, in the hospital, or in the mortuary. This place is where there is a deep exchange with a child, where one hand reaches out for another, where one stands quietly hearing news of one's own death, or where one witnesses a dear friend bravely bearing his suffering. The practice of expanded awareness is free to engage.

My love for Zen's stark truth touched me again when Myogen Steve Stucky, a close colleague who was abbot of San Francisco Zen Center, announced his impending death from stage 4 pancreatic cancer. Myogen and all of us needed Zen as a way to turn toward his suffering, imminent death, and our loss. Unlike my encounter with Olivia, I didn't know what to say in response to Myogen's explicit email foretelling his rapidly approaching death. Like many others, after a while I offered support and a request to visit. There were many such requests as the Zen community faced his dwindling days. Later, when I reiterated my request to his assistant, I was told there was a long list, that "a process had been put in place."

Facing my disappointment squarely, I said goodbye to the sky that contained us both, and I resolved to send a gift. As I was taught by my Japanese Zen teacher Fukushima Roshi, generosity means giving people actual gifts—giving more than just kindness and Dharma words. Fukushima Roshi explained that his own teacher, Zenkei Shibayama had taught him the importance of what could be passed hand to hand. Roshi had given me his calligraphy, cookies, books, pottery, and a rakusu—but he gave all in passing. It was understated, all given as we said goodbye. All was passed hand to hand, tenderly and personally.

Remembering how affected I had been by this precious Zen teaching of giving, I considered a specific gift for Myogen. I ruled out just a card, chocolates, or a book. It needed to be a direct taste of our mutual practice. Aha, Kyoto green tea—*Gyokuro* is an extravagant, flavorful, and naughtily expensive refreshment that we had enjoyed together on our breaks during our Zen team teaching.

Even the tea contained the tears of loss and endurance. Sadly, our favorite and go-to Japanese tea company had lost its field after 130 years of growing Uji tea and selling it in Kyoto. It was one among the many losses following Japan's 2011 tsunami. After considerable effort, I reestablished a tea contact I had met while practicing in Japan. With our new Gyokuro samples recently shipped from Japan, Myogen, Chikudo Lew Richmond, Enji Angie Boissevain, and I tasted the even more delicious, even naughtier, and even more expensive tea samples I had requested from our new vendor.

There was *Muratake* (Bamboo Forest), *Momoe* (One Hundred Blossoms), and *Otowa* (The Sound of Wings). Myogen quickly and definitively chose while the rest of us lingered over tasting. "The Sound of Wings," he pronounced as the winning tea. Was it premonitory, did he hear and taste the sound of his own wings? Remembering his choice fluttered my heart. I labeled a bag of "The Sound of Wings" and bowed my silent goodbye as it flew away from my Central Valley zendo to Myogen's home in the North Bay.

A week later my phone rang. It was Myogen. Ironically, he asked *me* if I had *time* to talk. Did I have time? I was painfully reminded that it was his time that was so preciously slipping away. Slightly breathless, I gathered my presence and affirmed that I had time to talk. He thanked me for the tea and asked if I could help him with his student Koshin Christine Palmer's Dharma transmission ceremony. Through Dharma transmission, Christine would become a fully independent teacher. I had mentored Christine in her training to become a leader in Myogen's Dharma Zen Center. Myogen struggled to find the words for what I might become to her. "She will be fully independent, a Dharma heir like you," he said, "but still she will need . . ." His words trailed off. Was it that he couldn't bear losing Christine, not being her teacher? Or was he afraid I would try to exert too much authority, not recognizing her independence? I supplied the word *consultant* to Myogen, but later, when Myogen brought up my ceremonial role as preceptor, Christine happily chirped, "Yes, Grace is my auntie." Another reason I love Zen. I got to be Christine's auntie, a much warmer relationship than consultant.

His illness had shocked all of us (he was the healthy one), and it urgently pushed him toward his own practice. When visiting Myogen for the ceremony, I found reminder notes posted on his easy chair: "I am of the nature of sickness," "I am of the nature of old age," "I am of the nature of death." Zen was alive and well in Myogen's home—the rubber meeting the road; the sticky notes on the easy chair, and my newly blossoming relationship as Christine's auntie.

Myogen and I spoke privately after the transmission ceremony, and he expressed his one remaining sadness—leaving his small grandchildren. He quoted, but did not sing, Bukka White's 1940 blues song "Fixin' to Die Blues," saying that he didn't mind dying but he sure hated to leave his children crying. Hearing his regret about his young grandchildren, I told Myogen Roshi what Olivia Roshi had taught me from her four-year-old perspective. Hearing Olivia's pronouncements, Myogen smiled his big enveloping smile and said, "Out of the mouths of babes." Leaving Myogen after Christine's Dharma transmission ceremony, knowing this would be our last earthly meeting, I touched his sleeve and said, "Don't forget what Olivia said. We'll be in touch."

And actually, we were in touch. He understood the tradition of Zen masters leaving their own final words or death poem. Myogen left this death poem for his mourners along with his body. The poem was made ready a few days before his passing and was posted on San Francisco Zen Center's website.

Death Poem
This human body truly is the entire cosmos
Each breath of mine, is equally one of yours, my darling
This tender abiding in "my" life
Is the fierce glowing fire of inner earth
Linking with all pre-phenomena
Flashing to the distant horizon
From "right here now" to "just this"
Now the horizon itself
Drops away—
Bodhi!
Svaha.
Myogen
12/27/13

Zen masters Olivia and Myogen helped me understand why I love Zen's facility for expanding awareness in close relationships. Let me count the ways being fully present enhances. Because we are present for each other; because we look for, find, and make meaning of our time together; because we have developed the presence to receive the message from our granddaughter about our own certain death; because we tell each other when we are afraid; because we listen to each other's fears; because we drink tea and hear "The Sound of (our own)

Wings"; because we help each other celebrate weddings, births, bar/bat mitzvahs, graduations, and funerals. Because we trust our awareness to take us to hospitals, prisons, schools, and homeless shelters. Because we grow food, we cook food, and we bring food to others when they cannot cook. Because we sew hems, alter clothing, complete robes for each other, even if we only wear them for our own cremation. Because we give friends and family, through our presence, our own death as a gift, as a poem, just as we have given our own life.

Oh, death poems are one more reason I love Zen. On a winter morning in 1360, Zen master Kozan Ichikyo gathered together his pupils. Kozan, age seventy-seven, told them that upon his death, they should bury his body, perform no ceremony, and hold no services in his memory. Sitting in the traditional Zen posture, he then wrote the following, which was published recently in the *Japan Times*:

> Empty-handed I entered
> the world
> Barefoot I leave it.
> My coming, my going—
> Two simple happenings
> That got entangled

I love being entangled in the Zen practice of awareness.

25

Yearning for My Urn

Bury My Ashes in Hagi-Yaki

All my spiritual training trips to Japan included shopping. Sometimes for toys for the play therapy groups I conducted for children, sometimes I shopped to actualize my own play therapy. My personal play developed my love for Japanese ceramics. I issued my warning to the population of Japan: "One day you will wake up and your entire country will be gone. I will have taken it home piece by piece in my suitcase." I recognized the irony of my craving for Japanese pottery juxtaposed with my intended quest to practice Zen as a way to let go of my attachments. I justified my art shopping as a spiritual purpose, but then there are many ways to fool oneself. But then again, if we completely follow our mind as it cavorts, we can realize all the teachings.

After more than a dozen trips to practice Zen in Japan, my well-honed shopping tastes focused on pottery. After pursuing and obtaining Bizen, Karatsu, Oribe, Raku, Asahi, Shigaraki, and Kutani wares, I became a devotee of Hagi and only Hagi ware. I developed one and only one pottery love, and it was Hagi-yaki (Hagi-style pottery). Hagi-yaki is a creamy white glaze that ages well with green tea and is soft enough to remind one of touching human skin. Purchasing the best Hagi-yaki required a trip to the old castle town of Hagi in Yamaguchi Prefecture. Luckily for me and my finances, this was not an easy trip. Getting to Hagi from the airport required two trains and a bus. If one arrived in Japan in the afternoon, the trip to Hagi needed to be broken up with an overnight along the way.

Because the trip to the town of Hagi was so complex and time consuming, I had determined that I would make this my last trip to Hagi, and that during this trip I would buy enough Hagi pottery to last me the rest of my life. For this trip, I had scheduled several days for touring and shopping in Hagi. On my first day, I realized that I could never achieve my goal of having enough Hagi-yaki—and certainly not in three days. Was it the Buddha or the Rolling Stones that declared there was no satisfaction to craving? Certainly the Buddha declared in the Four Noble Truths that craving was the source of suffering.

After one day of shopping, I glimpsed the truth of no satisfaction. No matter how much I shopped, I could never possess enough Hagi-yaki for this lifetime. In that moment, yet another craving-thought arose. I could "wear" Hagi-yaki in death. I then told my husband that I wanted my upcoming birthday gift to be a Hagi urn to contain my ashes—my cremated remains. Not surprisingly, my husband failed to see how romantic love would be expressed in this particular birthday gift. Nevertheless, he accepted that this gift suited my eccentric wishes even though it would not represent his romantic ideals.

The urn I chose to wear after my cremation ceremony is one of the most beautiful ceramic objects I have ever seen. Textured creamy white glaze with hints of pink, beautifully proportioned and multifaceted, with a gorgeous matching lid. The urn was well packed; and it returned home safely with me. Owning it and admiring it only fed my craving. Cravings are fickle, and I began to think about my afterlife in this gorgeous urn. The first anxious question to arise: After cremation, would I—as my ashes—fit in the urn? I was in possession of the ashes of one of my students. Her daughter was to retrieve them when her emotions allowed for the task. I went to look at the urn in which my student's remains now resided. Yes, I will fit in my urn, I concluded.

Shortly after that pang of doubt, I was hit by another. Would I be comfortable in my urn? It was awfully hard in there. I touched the smooth inside bottom of my urn with both admiration and concern. I considered my life in the potentially infinite hereafter and wondered about the wisdom of residing on such a hard surface. I decided that I could fashion a piece of foam to soften the bottom of my urn. With a sigh of relief, I looked forward to a cushy stay in my home after home-leaving. But shortly after my realization of cushiness, and in ongoing proof of the truth of the Buddha's and the Rolling Stones' no satisfaction, the next round of craving and its consequent suffering ensued.

What if I died at sea? What if my body parts were scattered in some way? What if I could never return to reside in my carefully chosen and exquisite urn? This horrible thought struck an arrow straight into my heart. What if I had nowhere to go, nowhere to be when I died? What if my much-loved Hagi urn and my remains (of what I thought of myself) would be separated at death? The dissolution of my Self became a little more real. I began to realize the foolishness of my cravings. I wasn't actually using the urn to prepare for my death. I was attempting to both control and deny the end of my life as I knew it.

I discussed my foolish worries with my son, Max—progressing through my litany of foolishness and arriving at the horror of being lost at sea. Max comforted me. "But, Mom, of course they will find something of you to put in the urn." I responded, "But, Max, that's not the point. My silliness is the point. I will be dead—what difference does it make?" I had realized that my urn would not save me, even if it would house "me"—or what was left of my physical remains. Awareness found its way to illuminate my ruminations on managing my own death.

Each of us must face the certainty and the uncertainty of our own death. While there are reasonable arrangements to make for the dispersal of one's assets or one's body, there is no solution to resolve the great mystery of when we transition from embodiment to our own body's nonexistence. Is there a wholesome way to face our certain departure at an uncertain date? My teacher Fukushima Roshi counseled that living fully was the way to prepare. He liked to say that we could not make a reservation for the journey in the same way we could make a reservation on the *shinkansen* (bullet train). His advice was to live life fully. Life is 99 percent of our experience; death is only 1 percent. We need to pay attention to the 99 percent. The 1 percent is inevitable, but we cannot plan that part of life.

At the end of his life, Fukushima Roshi described his terminal illness, Parkinson's disease, as his final koan. My husband asked him if he had solved this koan. He said, "I have, but I think there is a better answer." Working on koan with him while practicing at Tofukuji, he sometimes said to my koan presentation, "Okay, but there is a better answer." At the time of his illness, as he approached his death, he was still working on fully exploring the meaning of life. His awareness had developed into a capacity for considering the gravest problems.

The lesson is to learn from Fukushima Roshi's advice to live the 99 percent of life more fully. How do we live completely present until our moment of departure arrives? The Buddhist end-of-life-care pioneer Frank Ostaseski devotes his book *The Five Invitations* to a more detailed explanation of living that 99 percent by including the certainty of death as part of our life. Ostaseski also teaches full presence—not waiting until the end of life to expand our relationship with all beings and life in its myriad forms. This full presence allows us to welcome everything—to not hide our vulnerabilities. This advice is consistent with Ryokan's training for life and death. Ryokan, the eighteenth-century poet, expressed living fully in this poem from *Zen Bridge*:

> When a painful day is met,
> The painful day is met with welcome;
> At the time of death,
> Death is met with welcome.

The lesson my urn provided was that I could not control my death, but I could live fully, with gratitude and acceptance. And at the time of death, I could face death with the same state of mind. My awareness noticed that I was craving an afterlife in the urn. I was confusing acceptance of death with controlling my death. There are many ways to attempt to control death. You may be consumed with choosing a burial plot—one with the perfect view. You may decide, way in advance of a terminal illness, what conditions would be acceptable for continued medical effort and when you would choose to overdose on pain pills. You may seek to store a supply of pain pills or sleeping drugs—just to be prepared. All these fearful and controlling approaches are different than realistically choosing an advanced directive in case you can't make choices at the time of a health crisis. You need to watch your mind with the light of awareness shining on your struggle with death. Trust your awareness to watch your venture into the unknown. Are you facing the unknown or are you struggling to control what cannot be known?

One of my Zen students was in Hawaii when a mistaken Civil Defense warning blared out the approach of an imminent missile attack. She was at her hotel, in her nightgown, facing an instantaneous demise by a nuclear blast. She decided there was no time to find a place to hide and shelter from the potential explosion. She sent a loving text to her family, and she decided to sit on her balcony facing the luminous ocean. But before settling on the balcony, she decided to put on her clean underpants. She should be decent, out of respect for her family, in case her body was recovered. She was prepared to die enjoying the view while taking care of those who loved her in the only way available to her—clean underwear.

As Ryokan and Fukushima Roshi taught, cultivating appreciation of life is the way to live and to prepare for death. For my student, continuing to love and care for others was her path to living fully. She enjoyed sending a loving message to her family and looking at the ocean in what might have been her last moments. I may enjoy viewing a beautiful urn during my life, a daily reminder of beauty and impermanence. But if I think and hope the urn will ensure my safe travels and fashionable passage from this life to the next, my awareness assures me that I have become ensnared. Gripping my urn tightly, I lose the freedom and space in which I can freely create my life. It's better to hold it lightly.

References

Beck, Charlotte Joko. *Everyday Zen*. New York: HarperOne, 2007.

Christian Classics Ethereal Library (online). "True Hearing," *Meister Eckhart's Sermons IV*, www.ccel.org/ccel/eckhart/sermons.vii.html.

Cleary, Thomas, and J. C. Cleary, trans. *The Blue Cliff Record*. Boston: Shambhala Publications, 2005.

Dogen, Eihei, and Kosho Uchiyama. *From the Zen Kitchen to Enlightenment: Refining Your Life*. New York: Weatherhill, 1983.

Fukushima, Keido. *Zen Bridge: The Zen Teachings of Keido Fukushima*. Edited by Grace Schireson and Peter Schireson. Boston: Wisdom Publications, 2017.

Ikkyu Sojun. *Ikkyu and the Crazy Cloud Anthology: A Zen Poet of Medieval Japan*. Translated by Sonja Arntzen. Tokyo: University of Tokyo Press, 1987.

Ives, Christopher. *Zen Awakening and Society*. Honolulu: University of Hawaii Press, 1992.

Leighton, Taigen Dan. *Cultivating the Empty Field: The Silent Illumination of Zen Master Hongzhi*. North Clarendon, VT: Tuttle Publishing, 2000.

Master Dogen. *The Essential Dogen: Writings of the Great Zen Master*. Edited by Kazuaki Tanahashi and Peter Levitt. Boston: Shambhala Publications, 2013.

Master Joshu. *The Recorded Sayings of Zen Master Joshu*. Translated by James Green. Boston: Shambhala Publications, 2001.

Ostaseski, Frank. *The Five Invitations: Discovering What Death Can Teach Us about Living Fully*. New York: Flatiron Books, 2019.

Richardson, James. *Vectors: Aphorisms and Ten-Second Essays*. Keene, NY: Ausable Press, 2001.

Rumi, Jalal al-Din. *The Essential Rumi*. Translated by Coleman Barks. San Francisco: HarperOne, 2004.

San Francisco Zen Center. "January 2: Death Poem." Subtle Eye. January 2, 2014. http://subtleeye.sfzc.org/january-2.

Schireson, Grace. *Zen Women: Beyond Tea Ladies, Iron Maidens and Macho Masters*. Boston: Wisdom Publications, 2009.

Shibayama, Zenkei. *The Gateless Barrier: Zen Comments on the Mumonkan*. Boston: Shambhala Publications, 2000.

Suzuki, D. T. *Essays in Zen Buddhism*. New York: Grove Press, 1994.

Suzuki, Shunryu. *Zen Mind, Beginner's Mind*. Boston: Shambhala Publications, 2011.

Thacker, Eugene. "Black Illumination: Zen and the Poetry of Death." *Japan Times*, July 2, 2016. www.japantimes.co.jp/culture/2016/07/02/books/black-illumination-zen-poetry-death/#.XHqXIdF7lZI.

About the Author

Roshi Myōan Grace Jill Schireson, PhD, is a teacher in the Suzuki Roshi lineage empowered by Sojun Mel Weitsman, abbot of the Berkeley Zen Center. She has also practiced in the Rinzai tradition, and was encouraged to teach koans by Keido Fukushima Roshi, who was chief abbot of Tofukuji Monastery in Kyoto Japan. Grace is the author of *Zen Women: Beyond Tea Ladies, Iron Maidens, and Macho Masters,* and the co-editor of *Zen Bridge: The Zen Teachings of Keido Fukushima.* Grace is the head teacher of the Central Valley Zen Foundation and president of the Shogaku Zen Institute. She has founded several Zen groups in California and currently offers meditation instruction at Stanford University. Grace is also a clinical psychologist specializing in women and families. Married for fifty-one years, she has two sons and four grandchildren.